Testimonials for
PLAY YOUR BEST GOLF NOW

WHAT THE PROS SAY:

"Pia and Lynn are revolutionaries in the complex, overanalyzed world of golf instruction. They have the unique ability to provide individualized instruction based on the needs, strengths, and weaknesses of the student. They have helped transform my game, and more importantly, my life, to best support my passionate pursuit of my dreams and aspirations on the global golf stage. VISION54 is the best golf/sport/life/happiness program ever developed, bar none!" —Kevin Streelman, PGA Tour player

"Lynn and Pia have helped me learn how to more fully realize the joy and passion I have for the game of golf. They have shown me that magic is possible and that the only limit to what I can achieve on the golf course is my beliefs. If you believe in greatness you can make greatness happen." —Ai Miyazato, LPGA Tour player

"Pia and Lynn have helped me understand how I get the best out of myself and to better understand the game of golf. Through their coaching I have gotten to know myself better, know what to do to not get in my own way, and to allow myself to dream!"
—Suzann Pettersen, LPGA Tour player

"We share the same vision—that it's possible to birdie every hole and shoot 54, and that there are no limits to what you can achieve. In many ways, I am the embodiment of the VISION54 coaching philosophies." —Annika Sorenstam, LPGA superstar

"Pia and Lynn's simple approaches make me mentally a stronger player." —Yani Tseng, LPGA Tour player

"The week I started working with Lynn and Pia, I won! Their coaching has made my game more complete." —Na Yeon Choi, LPGA Tour player

"I thought I knew it all. I was wrong. I began with the smallest changes, and they made the biggest difference in my golf game and in my life. Thanks to Lynn and Pia, I fell in love with golf again." —Grace Park, LPGA Tour player

"Pia, Lynn, and their staff have been instrumental in my success in the past two years. Their insight into the golf game and the mind is second to none. I have reaped rewards from incorporating their techniques in the past and look forward to learning more in the future." —Brittany Lincicome, LPGA Tour player

"Pia and Lynn have set a new standard in mental coaching. It's amazing how they can pick up on the little things, tell me to try something different, and it actually works. When I work with them, everything seems to have a simple solution. I feel very fortunate to have been able to work with them." —Sophie Gustafson, LPGA Tour player

"VISION54 is a phenomenal concept. Its message is simple yet often overlooked: the fact that you can accomplish and do anything; the possibilities are endless and limitless. The concept of VISION54 is such a refreshing outlook on golf and life. Pia and Lynn are the most positive people I know, and the energy that they exude is amazing; they make you want to be better." —Brittany Lang, LPGA Tour player

"Pia and Lynn have helped me to get my focus specific, given me tools to enjoy learning in everyday practice, given me wings to dream big, supported me to experience things with my heart, and helped me to get my own spirit of the game stronger."

—Minea Blomqvist, LPGA Tour player

"The wisdom of Pia and Lynn has had a major impact on me as an athlete and as a person as well. The practical skills I have developed through their coaching and friendship have equipped me to be more effective in practice; competition, and away from the course."   —Jason Allred, PGA Tour player

WHAT THE WORLD'S BEST COACHES SAY:

"Pia and Lynn are dynamic, passionate, and very astute about the game of golf. Golfers always attempt to improve at the game through technique and equipment alone. What make Pia and Lynn so unique in instruction is that their emphasis is playing better golf with an effective game plan. Their ideas have helped me in my coaching of tour players. Apply their principles and you too will improve where it matters most: your score."

—Sean Foley, coach of several PGA Tour players

"I love Lynn and Pia because they understand and teach the game in all of its breadth. They are great coaches who work with the things that are important to all golfers as we try to score. There is more to golf than swinging, and *Play Your Best Golf Now* deals with it. You cannot go wrong in following VISION54."

—Dave Pelz, Dave Pelz Scoring Game Schools

"Pia Nilsson and Lynn Marriott have revolutionized modern golf coaching worldwide. Learn and apply the unique performance and scoring drills and skills outlined in this book. You'll play better golf and have more fun."

—Henry Brunton, Canadian National Team coach

"I have known Pia Nilsson and Lynn Marriott for many years. Their passion for the game is second to none. The VISION54 approach is far more than just pure golf technique; it allows an individual to unlock their true potential by opening their mind and believing anything is possible to achieve. Golf games and, more importantly, the game of life, benefit through their teachings."

—David Leadbetter, David Leadbetter Golf Academy

"Lynn and Pia have created a variety of effective ways to rid golfers of the interference that restricts on-course performance. The bonus is that these techniques also help you reach your full potential in life, too. Simply put, they are among the most influential coaches in the world today. You will only get better incorporating their ideas."

—Mike Bender, 2009 PGA Teacher of the Year

"Lynn and Pia deliver results. Their complete game coaching at VISION54 makes a big difference in players' games, from PGA Tour pros to 30-handicap players."

—Michael Breed, PGA head golf professional at Sunningdale Country Club, host of *The Golf Fix* on the Golf Channel.

"You can have the greatest golf swing in the world, but you might not be able to break 80. Lynn and Pia get it. They understand there is much more to peak performance than just ball striking. This wonderful game has many pieces, and they do a marvelous job of putting those pieces together for your best performance on the golf course."

—Randy Smith, PGA head golf professional at Royal Oaks Country Club, Dallas, Texas; 2002 PGA Teacher of the Year

"Lynn and Pia's reputation for helping golfers improve is well deserved. *Play Your Best Golf Now* is another example of their understanding of both the nature of golf and human nature. It is filled with insights that any golfer, professional or amateur, will find useful."
—Michael Hebron, PGA Master Professional and 1991 PGA Teacher of the Year

"Pia and Lynn are two of golf's brightest thinkers and hardest workers. They never stop trying to improve on their past success, a trait of great coaches. They have helped countless golfers lower their scores and enjoy the game. If you follow their advice, you can do the same. I heartily recommend you apply what you read. You won't regret it."   —Martin Hall, 2008 PGA Teacher of the Year

"There are a lot of distractions surrounding tournament golf. Lynn and Pia do a great job teaching their students how to focus on game days."   —Stan Utley, coach of many PGA Tour players

"Pia, Lynn, and I have shared quite a few clients over the years, some of them the top-ranked players in the world. I have seen their results firsthand and can say with the utmost confidence that this book will help you achieve whatever goals you might have in this great game of golf."
        —Kevin Smeltz, worldwide director of training and certification, David Leadbetter Golf Academy

"What Lynn and Pia are doing in golf is really not that special. They just have that skill to take what has been made very complicated and turn it into something really simple. In today's world, that is obviously completely unique, and it's probably why they have come to revolutionize golf coaching and so many players' approach to performing on the course. I suggest you read this book quickly, and ideally before you waste another four hours on the golf course with the wrong approach!"

—Peter Mattsson, director of coaching, English Golf Union

"Pia and Lynn provide valuable information for players or coaches seeking to become the best they can be. They break down the complexity of performance in golf into the 'need to know' essentials."

—David Colclough, head of member education, British PGA

"Lynn and Pia have positively influenced my playing and coaching by providing me relevant educational experiences in areas that I had not previously thought of. If you want to improve your golf game or coaching, do yourself a favor and attend their programs and read their books."

—Rudy Duran, PGA Life Member and first golf coach of Tiger Woods

"The VISION54 concept has given me all the tools I needed for successful coaching. Pia and Lynn have inspired me to coach each person as a human being, as well as a player or fellow coach."

—Walle Danewid, former head coach, Swedish National Teams

"These two ladies have gotten a head start on golf's final frontier. They get past the swing minutiae and help their players play better golf. They are the best!"

—Chuck Cook, *Golf Digest* Top 50 teacher, 1996 PGA Teacher of the Year

"Pia Nilsson and Lynn Marriott rank among the most accomplished golf teachers in the world. Their record of producing star players and helping other teachers to do so as well is impressive. If you want to improve your game, read this book . . . NOW!"

—Dr. Gary Wiren, PGA Hall of Fame

"From a teaching perspective I have watched and listened to Lynn and Pia over the last fifteen years, and they have created a very comprehensive but simple approach to getting the most out of their students, without complicating the process. Those who want to reach their potential should apply their ideas."

—Mike Malaska, *Golf Digest* Top 50 teacher

WHAT GOLF EXECUTIVES SAY:

"Pia Nilsson and Lynn Marriott understand athletes, understand competition, and have the unique ability to get the absolute best out of the players on tour. Having read *Every Shot Must Have a Purpose* and having seen so many players on the LPGA embrace its principles, I couldn't wait to read *Play Your Best Golf Now!*"

—Michael Whan, LPGA commissioner

"Lynn and Pia inherently believe that every person can maximize their potential. Whether you're the number-one player in the world, or a weekend golfer looking to discover your best game, the holistic approach of VISION54 will not only coach you to be better, it will make you love this sport even more."

—Cindy L. Davis, president, Nike Golf

"If you want to develop skills that will help you perform better both in golf and in life, then Lynn and Pia have a proven track record of helping players of all ages, skill levels, and walks of life. At The First Tee, we have benefited from their expertise and so will you!"

—Joe Louis Barrow, Jr., chief executive officer, The First Tee

"Lynn Marriott and Pia Nilsson have been selflessly sharing their unique insights into the learning and teaching of golf with other

PGA professionals. Their presentations consistently rank high in their content and delivery by the experts in golf instruction."

—Joe Steranka, chief executive officer, PGA of America

"Pia Nilsson and Lynn Marriott are not only two of the finest teachers in golf, they are also two of the finest people I know."

—Ty M. Votaw, executive vice president, PGA Tour

"The insights and lessons of VISION54 extend well beyond the practice range and the golf course: Focus on what you can control, stay in the moment, and revel in the joy of playing. These are very valuable lessons for life!"

—Rear Admiral Marty Evans, U.S. Navy (Ret.); former CEO, Girl Scouts of the USA and American Red Cross

"Play Your Best Golf Now is the third instruction book from Pia Nilsson and Lynn Marriott. Any golfer with an eye on improving their game needs to own this excellent trilogy."

—Barney Adams, founder, Adams Golf

"Lynn Marriott and Pia Nilsson have helped countless golfers—ranging from those just starting out to the very best in the world—play to their maximum with their innovative teaching skills. Above that is their sheer passion for the game and for life, which is immediately evident the very moment you are in the ladies' company. Let them help YOU!"

—Ken Schofield, executive director, PGA European Tour, 1975–2004

"Lynn Marriott and Pia Nilsson have cracked the code on how to communicate with golfers of all ages and abilities. Anyone who is serious about improving their game should read *Play Your Best Golf Now.*" —Steve Mona, chief executive officer, World Golf Foundation

"I can think of no better source than Pia and Lynn when it comes to preparation to play the game of golf. Their knowledge and experience certainly qualify them as leaders in their field."

—Dana Garmany, chairman and CEO, Troon Golf

"All that changes in our very physical being is a reflection of the complex workings of the mind. Pia and Lynn help us channel those workings to make what we do better."

—Frank Thomas, USGA technical director, 1974-2000; founder of Frankly Golf

"Having read much of their teachings, our expectations were high, but were still far exceeded in person. Their combination of logic, order, intelligence, and spirituality is at once irrefutable, confidence-inspiring, and soothing. We went for help in how to approach golf, but like so many things in this great game, it turned out to be a lesson in life."

—Seth Waugh, chief executive officer, Deutsche Bank Americas

"In working with Lynn and Pia I was delighted to experience their mastery at coaching human potential and achieving extraordinary performance in golf and life. Their belief and work with integrating the physical, mental, and emotional through intention and practice is a model for the future."

—Michael Murphy, author of *Golf in the Kingdom*; cofounder, Esalen Institute

"Lynn Marriott and Pia Nilsson are two of the best communicators we have in the teaching industry, and it is reflected in their energy and unselfishness to share their knowledge with their peers. Their latest collaboration in print, *Play Your Best Golf Now*, reflects their insight into how we all can take the next step to improving our game."

—Brian Whitcomb, former president, PGA of America

WHAT THE GOLF WRITERS SAY:

"Pia and Lynn are the superstars of golf instruction in the twenty-first century. They're not just teaching us arm angles and swing planes—they focus on the total experience. What you achieve is limited in large part by what you believe you can achieve. Pia and Lynn inspire their students to dream big. They remind us that the passion and joy are as important to low scores as mechanics. The genius of VISION54 is that it's compatible with any swing theory."

—Jerry Tarde, chairman and editor-in-chief, *Golf Digest*

"If you want to improve your golf game so you can hold your own with thieves, this is the book for you."

—Dan Jenkins, award-winning author and *Golf Digest* columnist

"Pia and Lynn have a knack for lasering in on tactics that help golfers get better efficiently, while avoiding those that seem useful but mostly are a waste of time. Their approach isn't the same old, same old. It's fresh, and for those who believe (like me) and are willing to make an honest effort, it really works."

—John Paul Newport, golf columnist, *The Wall Street Journal*

"What Pia and Lynn do so well is tap into the golfer who resides in all of us—the player who is in the moment, peaceful, trusting, and accepting. In many ways, they teach us how to be our own best friend on the golf course. Even better, the skills can be applied to any aspect of life."

—Damon Hack, senior writer, golf and NFL, *Sports Illustrated*

"The positive vibe of Lynn Marriott and Pia Nilsson is palpable, whether face-to-face or in the words of their books. If you want to feed off the basic principles that made Annika Sorenstam the best mind in the women's game, if you want to start smiling on the golf course again, then let Lynn and Pia set you free."
—Tim Rosaforte, senior writer, *Golf World*; analyst, Golf Channel and NBC

"If you know golfers who think they've tried it all and nothing works, give them one of Pia and Lynn's books. They'll discover new ways to get better. Pia and Lynn look at all of the golfer's opportunities to improve, not at creating the so-called perfect swing. And they make it fun."   —Peter Morrice, senior editor, *Golf Digest*

"Several LPGA players have met with a VISION54 instructor for the first time on a Tuesday and by Sunday, they're hoisting a trophy. That kind of result gets attention. Yet no one on tour is a better walking billboard for the VISION54 program than Ai Miyazato, who credits her five victories in 2010 to a complete mental turnaround."   —Beth Ann Baldry, senior writer, *Golfweek*

"What I think matters most to good players and others is Pia and Lynn's ability to make you really like the game and the challenges again. Some have a continuing love affair, but not everyone."
          —Judy Rankin, World Golf Hall of Fame member, TV analyst

"Pia Nilsson and Lynn Marriott are on the cutting edge of the very best teaching in golf. Their philosophy is fresh and inviting; their success is indisputable. If you want to play better golf, listen to them."   —Christine Brennan, sports columnist, *USA Today*

WHAT GOLF RESEARCHERS SAY:

"When it comes to improving your game, Lynn and Pia and all the experts at VISION54 are the real deal. Coaching golfers to reach their best takes a lot more than knowing how to swing a club. Their techniques are simple, effective, and proven with all levels of players. Do yourself and your game a favor, and read this book."   —Dr. Greg Rose, cofounder, Titleist Performance Institute

"Lynn and Pia are highly respected, nationally and internationally recognized leaders in the golf teaching and coaching profession. Their teaching, coaching, VISION54 program, and two previous books are all on the cutting edge, just as their new book, *Play Your Best Golf Now*, promises to be."
                    —Dr. Bob Christina, dean emeritus and professor, University of
                    North Carolina at Greensboro

"Whenever I see a player making rapid progress on a professional tour, I wonder if they are being coached by Nilsson and Marriott. I have been surprised to discover how often this is the case. Lynn and Pia clearly have an approach that is both unique and powerful. In *Play your Best Golf Now* they share more of their insights and practices that can make every golfer a better player."
                    —Dr. Paul G. Schempp, director, Sport Instruction Research Lab,
                    University of Georgia

"Lynn and Pia and their VISION54 have developed a most unique program. Whether you attend their clinics or read their books, you know you are learning more than golf; you are learning skills that you can apply in all areas of your life. Golf is just the vehicle they use to teach the skills. All you need to do is to step back and make sure you see the big picture that they are helping you create."
                    —Steven J. Danish, PhD, professor of Psychology and Social and
                    Behavioral Health

"Over the thirty years I have known Pia and the fifteen years I have known Lynn, I have yet to find more industrious students of the game and life. They both have a unique and creative way of applying knowledge from many areas of research and experience to help individuals discover their own best performance. It has been an honor to know and work with them."

—Debbie Crews Ketterling, PhD, faculty research associate, Arizona State University

"Life is full of surprises and very few of us get to where we want to go. However, those who have a passion for what they do always succeed and pull others along with them. In my mind, that is the very essence of a coach. Pia and Lynn are true coaches. They have a passion for life and for golf, and their words and life experiences will help any level of golfer aspire to be the best they can be."

—Dave Phillips, cofounder, Titleist Performance Institute

PLAY YOUR BEST GOLF NOW

PLAY YOUR BEST GOLF NOW

DISCOVER VISION54'S
8 ESSENTIAL PLAYING SKILLS

Pia Nilsson and Lynn Marriott
with Ron Sirak

GOTHAM
BOOKS

GOTHAM BOOKS
Published by Penguin Group (USA) Inc.
375 Hudson Street, New York, New York 10014, U.S.A.
Penguin Group (Canada), 90 Eglinton Avenue East, Suite 700, Toronto, Ontario M4P 2Y3,
Canada (a division of Pearson Penguin Canada Inc.); Penguin Books Ltd, 80 Strand, London
WC2R 0RL, England; Penguin Ireland, 25 St Stephen's Green, Dublin 2, Ireland (a division
of Penguin Books Ltd); Penguin Group (Australia), 250 Camberwell Road, Camberwell,
Victoria 3124, Australia (a division of Pearson Australia Group Pty Ltd); Penguin Books India
Pvt Ltd, 11 Community Centre, Panchsheel Park, New Delhi—110 017, India; Penguin
Group (NZ), 67 Apollo Drive, Rosedale, Auckland 0632, New Zealand (a division of Pearson
New Zealand Ltd); Penguin Books (South Africa) (Pty) Ltd, 24 Sturdee Avenue, Rosebank,
Johannesburg 2196, South Africa

Penguin Books Ltd, Registered Offices: 80 Strand, London WC2R 0RL, England

Published by Gotham Books, a member of Penguin Group (USA) Inc.

First printing, May 2011
10 9 8 7 6 5 4 3 2 1

Gotham Books and the skyscraper logo are trademarks of Penguin Group (USA) Inc.

LIBRARY OF CONGRESS CATALOGING-IN-PUBLICATION DATA
has been applied for.

ISBN 978-1-592-40626-5

Printed in the United States of America
Set in Bembo and Calvert
Designed by Sabrina Bowers

To all the players we have coached, who keep us curious, motivated, and evolving as coaches.
—L.M. and P.N.

For Castle Hills Golf Course, where it all began.
—R.S.

Contents

INTRODUCTION

Find Yourself in the Game

"May your heart always be joyful, may your song always be sung, may you stay forever young."

Songwriter Bob Dylan

By Ron Sirak

J immy Cannon, a writer I grew up reading, once said: "Sportswriters are underpaid and overprivileged." What Jimmy meant is that sportswriters have the privilege of a ringside seat for genius; we get a firsthand glimpse of greatness. That's a real treat and also a real challenge. We get to watch amazing things happen and then we try to communicate that wonder to those who weren't there. The skill and diligence of the writer influences that communication, but success is also affected a great deal by access. The more immersed you are in a situation, the more effectively you can tell others what happened.

As a journalist, I spend much of my life peering through a bubble at the lives and achievements of others. On rare occasions, entry is gained to the bubble and I can swim in the story—live it, breathe it and feel it, let it wash over me. Such good fortune came to me with Lynn Marriott, Pia Nilsson and their unique approach to golf instruction called VISION54. At first, I was writing about them and learning their method. Then they asked me in, and I saw up close how effectively their approach to golf works. It was a life-changing moment and the beginning of a never-ending journey of discovery.

To think of Lynn and Pia as great *golf* teachers is to do them a disservice: They are much more than that. They are brilliant *life* teachers. **VISION54 is not only a blueprint for great golf; it is a road map for how to live an organized, efficient and fulfilling life.** The title of this book is *Play Your Best Golf Now*, but it could just as accurately be called *Live Your Best Life Now*. VISION54 is a holistic approach to creating a harmonious life, and a happier person plays better golf. Lynn and Pia make achieving peak performance a believable goal, and the tools you learn from them in this book make it attainable.

Quite simply, your golf game needs this book. The 8 Essential Playing Skills introduced here are essential to *the* game and to *your* game. Lynn and Pia take the mystery and intimidation out of the skills of golf. They make those skills accessible. You will learn how to add those skills to your game so you can play better golf. **YOU will take ownership of YOUR game and become less vulnerable to the latest gadget or swing fad that comes down the pike.**

Lynn and Pia take the magical concept of peak performance and make it attainable. They make peak performance real and they make it possible for your game.

In the 8 Essentials, you will find a doorway to better play and you will find a platform upon which you can stand to reach your full potential. Instead of hoping for great performance, this book is your blueprint for realizing it, helping you to build a practice program for playing your best golf and allowing you to truly believe that great golf will happen because of the 8 Essential Playing Skills. That belief is a crucial component of achievement. You will learn how to get the most out of the swing you have and out of the skill you possess. You will learn how to become the best possible you. Through the 8 Essentials you will shoot lower scores without changing your swing, and you will learn how to make good golf happen for you.

Unless you have a baseline of competence in the 8 Essentials, you will never fully realize how well you can swing the club and stroke the ball with the technique you have right now. And isn't that what you want: to be the best you, not try to be someone else? This is a template for a complete view of the game of golf. **These 8 Essentials will enable you to learn how to make your swing show up and hold up on the golf course—where it matters.** VISION54 is about doing, not just thinking about doing. Lynn and Pia move beyond overintellectualized instruction and make golf a sport again—a game you play.

One of the aspects of VISION54 that has become my personal mantra for dealing not just with golf but with just about everything else in life is this: "We can't control what happens to us, but we can control how we react to what happens to us." That's not something I am always good at, and it is an attitude I have to constantly work to build. I tend to personalize events. Now when I have a setback on the golf course or at work or in the motor vehicles bureau, I sing to myself: "It's not just me, it's life and life only."

We all get bad bounces. There is comfort in understanding that. We all have bad things happen to us. What you will learn from Lynn and Pia is how to handle those bad bounces in a way that will not imprint bad behavior in your memory so that it will affect your future actions. We can make a better future for ourselves by learning to control how we react to the present. Great golf is about repeatability of the swing, and in this book you will learn how to repeat the good things about your game and not the bad. The 8 Essential Playing Skills are not just for golf; they are for all you do.

One of the many times I was at Lynn and Pia's school, they asked me which of the Essentials I thought had had the biggest impact on my game. When I considered what happens when my game goes wrong, I realized that I get out of balance, usually in making the transition from the backswing to the downswing. That was a huge realization for me. Now, as part of my warm-up, I hit shots standing on one leg, with my feet together, and with one arm.

The purpose of these exercises is to slow down my swing and keep me in balance. These exercises also build a level of trust within me for my swing. And like others you will hear from in this book, I can say this without any hesitation: "It works." Now when I practice, I spend the bulk of my time working on improving and maintaining my balance. And that is another part of what you will learn in this book—the 2 Practice Essentials, or how to maximize your return on the time you invest in practice. Lynn and Pia break down the barriers between practice and golf, making the two one glorious game.

By the time we finished this book, players with whom Lynn and Pia have worked had won more than one hundred professional tournaments, and five of them had captured major championships. Quite literally, thousands of professional golfers read our first book, *Every Shot Must Have a Purpose*, as well as our book on practice, *The Game Before the Game*. Some of the most prominent swing coaches in the world have asked Lynn and Pia to work with their students. Some of the most prominent players, when they saw the success of VISION54 students, approached Lynn and Pia for help.

Anyone who meets Lynn and Pia and is exposed to their vision of golf and their view of life comes away not only impressed but also convinced that they are truly on to something. You cannot help but be swept up by their enthusiasm for golf. The thousands of players who have attended their school at the Legacy Golf Resort in Phoenix and at other clubs around the world have become their best salespeople.

Those people go home, play their best golf ever and, when asked by their friends why they are playing so well, tell them about VISION54.

There is a revolution going on in the way golf is being taught, and Lynn and Pia are in the vanguard of that movement. Many teachers are recognizing that golf is about much more than arm angles and swing slots, and those instructors recognize the contributions of Lynn and Pia. In a vote of their peers, Pia was named the number-one female golf instructor and Lynn was number two. Both are *Golf Digest* Top 50 instructors. *Golf Magazine* ranked their school number one in the nation. They have developed an approach to golf that enhances any swing theory and maximizes any skill level.

Lynn and Pia will help you learn how to live life, not watch it. When it comes to golf, you will learn not only how to swing the club better but how to play the game better—how to get the ball into the hole sooner. And you will learn how to enjoy the game more. **This book takes the mystery and intimidation out of a very challenging game**. In these pages, you will learn the skills needed to play your best more often.

It has been my great privilege and good fortune to get to know Lynn and Pia and to learn the teachings of VISION54. They have improved my golf game, they have improved my work as a writer, and they have improved my life. Now you have that privilege too. You have an opportunity to learn how to Play Your Best Golf Now. Enjoy!

PLAY YOUR BEST GOLF NOW

CHAPTER 1

Grow Your Vision of Greatness

"If you have to ask what jazz is, you'll never know."
Trumpeter Louis Armstrong

SWING KEY: Be your own best coach; you are the expert on you.

Golf is a living relationship between the game and you. To play great golf is not merely a matter of mastering a series of mechanical moves, but also the art of surrendering to the sweet choreography of the dance you share with the game. At the heart of the VISION54 philosophy is the notion that great golf springs from that intricate relationship. **The key to great performance has as much to do with passion, belief and trust as it does with arm angles, body positions and swing planes.** You are not a golfer who happens to be a person, but rather a person who happens to play golf.

Also at the heart of our thinking is the notion that

everything—including schools of thought—grows, evolves and matures. This book represents not just the further refinement of the approach we described in *Every Shot Must Have a Purpose* and *The Game Before the Game*, this book also gives you specific tools we have developed to use in your pursuit of greatness on the golf course: the 8 Essential Playing Skills for Peak Performance—the EPS that is your GPS for golf—and the 2 Essential Practice Skills that will enable you to integrate the 8 Essentials into your game in the most efficient way.

What is VISION54? **It is our belief that what you achieve is greatly affected by what you believe you can achieve.** Why make it your goal to par every hole? Why not make it your mission to birdie every hole—and shoot a 54! We want you to approach life with the attitude that anything is possible. We want you to go from the kind of one-dimensional thinking that creates paralysis by analysis on the golf course to the kind of multidimensional experiences that will help you play better. We want you to realize your potential. The ideas we touched upon in our first two books are amplified here. In these pages, you will find the skills needed to realize this vision.

VISION54 will expand your belief in what's possible. As that belief strengthens, you will create a personalized road map that leads you to being a better player—your MY54—based on your experience with the game. You will also determine what keeps you from reaching your full potential. This is your NOT54—the bad habits and tendencies you have developed that consistently cause you to get in your own way. As you learn to distinguish between what is and what is not under your control, you will play better golf. Control what you can and let go of what you can't.

The 8 Essential Playing Skills are the tools you need to realize VISION54. Through our first book, *Every Shot Must Have a Purpose*, players and teachers began to understand the importance of VISION54, and to realize the benefits of having a broader understanding of the game of golf. But many also felt lost, unsure of where to even begin the journey. The 8 Essentials in this book are the bricks needed for building a foundation of skills that lead you to becoming a better player. *Every Shot Must Have a Purpose* was the revelation; *Play Your Best Golf Now* is the realization.

Certainly, the fundamentals of the game are important to master: grip, stance, posture, etc. But there is more than one correct way to swing a golf club, and we feel the traditional list of fundamentals does not go far enough. We are not subtracting from the conventional wisdom about golf—or questioning it—but rather adding to it and expanding its vision. Success in golf, like any other activity, involves making clear, committed decisions and carrying that commitment with you when it comes time to act. In golf, that action is striking the ball. This it not negotiable; it is essential. You must commit to every shot. Every great player will tell you this is true.

You have hit good golf shots with your swing; you have hit great shots with your swing. **Lower scores result from**

the repeatability of your swing when it is at its best.
The Essential Playing Skills will enable you to repeat your best
swing more often and hit good shots more often. Along the
way, you will rediscover your love of the game, deepen your
understanding of it and ultimately enjoy golf more. Remember, it is a *game* and you do *play* it. Don't fear the shot, live it!

In our decades of work with players of all skill levels, we
have come to understand the components that are absolutely
essential to success in golf. We have distilled these 8 Essential Playing Skills from the hundreds of factors influencing
your swing and game. When you have learned the Essentials,
you will integrate them into your game to complement the
technical and physical skills you already possess. Learning the
Essentials gives you a starting template for a more complete
game. One of the things we have learned from all of the golfers we have seen through the years is that the 8 Essentials
maximize the return on your investment of the time you put
into golf.

The 8 Essential Playing Skills

1. **Leave your mind behind:** This is about entering the Play
   Box, the sacred ground of golf. Learn to engage with the
   shot. Just make it happen.

2. **Decide and commit:** Become a more confident player by
   learning to make clear decisions that you trust and stick
   with. Believe in great golf.

3. **Find your balance:** Walk the tightrope to great play. Be centered physically and mentally.

4. **Feel your tempo and dance to its rhythm:** Learn how your natural tempo feels and discover what tempo works best for you.

5. **Tame tension:** There is no greater saboteur of the golf swing than tension. Recognize it and manage it. Balance, tempo and tension awareness (BTT) will make any swing better.

6. **Build emotional resilience:** Learn how to turn disappointing results into stepping stones rather than stumbling blocks.

7. **Store memories:** File away the good and neutralize the bad. The past doesn't have to be your future. You can learn from the past to make a better present.

8. **Drown self-talk in useful thoughts:** Hear that voice in your head that raises doubts and fears? We all have it. Have a dialogue with it. That voice isn't always right. You can set it straight.

In this book you will find exercises that will help you to master the 8 Essentials. Through those exercises you will build a toolbox of skills that will make you more consistent in your performance and more confident in your execution of the golf swing. Remember, peak performance does not have to be an accidental state that you stumble upon only rarely. Instead, it should be an intentional destination you can learn how to access more frequently.

The 2 Essential Practice Skills:

1. **Simulate golf:** The time and effort you invest in practice yields the best return when it is most like real golf. Make practice like golf by inviting the pressure of performing onto the practice range with you. This is crucial to getting better.

2. **Integrate skills:** Why are you practicing? Don't just hit balls, practice with a purpose. Have a plan. Hit each shot with an objective in mind.

There are many people who hit golf balls for an hour and think they have practiced golf, when all they have done is hit golf balls for an hour. The Essential Practice Skills involve practicing with a purpose. The Essential Playing Skills involve playing with a purpose. Success is built upon integrating these skills into your game. **Our goal is to tear down the walls between practice and play, between theory and performance.** We want you to learn not to be afraid of a golf shot but rather to be inspired by the challenge. This can only be achieved by experiencing real golf in practice—not by mindlessly scraping and hitting balls on the range.

FROM THINK BOX TO PLAY BOX

We see the process of hitting a golf shot as a two-step activity, divided between the Think Box and the Play Box, and separated by an imaginary Decision Line. The Think Box is where you formulate your plan for the shot you are about to hit. The Play Box is where you execute that plan. Our observations have led us to realize that for many players, the Think Box has become a clutter of pre-shot routines—practice swings, overthinking, etc. We have found through trial and error that simplifying your Think Box routine helps to create a stronger state of Decision and Commitment. This way, you are able to step into the Play Box with the kind of trust you need to hit a successful shot. By making clear decisions and committing fully to those decisions, you will create a stronger sense of engagement and a more vibrant energy for the real moment of truth—executing the shot in the Play Box.

We view this book as a celebration of the most sacred ground of golf—that moment when you cross the *Decision Line* from the *Think Box* into the *Play Box* to hit a golf shot. Our purpose is to help you perform better on the golf course—where it matters—and not on the practice range, where most players leave their best shots. **We want your game to show up and hold up on the golf course.** Through the first-person accounts in this book by players of all skill levels who have been helped by VISION54, you will learn the secrets needed to Play Your Best Golf Now.

One of the joyous things about golf is that it is a highly individualized sport, while at the same time being extremely social. In what other athletic activity can playing partners, or even opponents, spend time walking and talking together while competing? In what other sport is the venue on which the game is played as much a part of the experience as the game itself? In what other game can players of varied skill levels compete against one another as equals? It is important to incorporate that physical, social and spiritual connection into how you approach golf. This game is far too beautiful to be reduced to just swing theory. Immerse yourself in golf, become one with it and then watch your scores drop.

At the core of the beauty of the game is the understanding that golf is an integrated and a holistic experience in which you celebrate your uniqueness in an extremely social setting. It's an individual activity played out on a collective stage. **Golf presents the same challenges as life: finding and preserving your identity amid outside pressure to be someone else.** Central to VISION54 is the belief that you will play your best golf when you are being most true to yourself, when you have integrated who you are with how you play.

We are baffled when we see people overlook their own unique character as they try to learn the game. Often, in searching for answers, players try to become someone else—swing like someone else, think like someone else, behave like someone else—rather than pursue their full potential by learning to be themselves.

Not everyone swings like Mickey Wright, nor should they, and not everyone thinks like Ben Hogan, nor should they. Part of what makes Tiger Woods a great player is that he is totally himself on the golf course, right down to his occasional expletives that go uncensored. Woods knows that to break the records of Jack Nicklaus he need not try to become the Golden Bear, but rather must find his own Tiger. He embraces his unique spirit of the game.

Our approach acknowledges, first and foremost, that you are an individual. We don't teach you, we help you learn. In a world cluttered with a myriad of specialized instructors, we view ourselves as coaches of the complete game of golf. Our emphasis is on first-person experience rather than third-person observation. We are not offering a gimmicky quick fix—although some of our students have seen astonishingly fast results—but rather a permanent foundation for greatness, a functional baseline for long-term excellence that will last as long as you play the game.

We do not want to teach you someone else's swing; we want you to learn to find your own. **Because of this approach, VISION54 is compatible with any swing theory, with any personality and with any skill level. It will make anyone better.** We help our students enhance their performance, in part, by enabling them to enjoy the game more. We do this by helping you learn the tools that tame tension, reduce self-doubt and lead to full commitment. You can't play your best when you are playing scared. Whatever your approach to the game, the Essential Playing Skills will help you get more out of it.

In our previous books, we established the framework of the VISION54 philosophy for play and practice. This book reflects the continued maturation of that thought process. You will learn about the *physical*, *technical*, *mental*, *emotional* and *social* elements of the game, but you will also learn how those components exist as overlapping circles of experience within the larger circle representing the *spirit of the game*. Those elements defined in our earlier works will become accessible to you through the skills you will learn from this book.

Having a great swing is not playing great golf. That is only part of the puzzle of peak performance. Our goal is to unify the elements of a game that have become splintered into swing coaches, long-game coaches, short-game coaches, putting coaches, mind coaches and more. **We are performance coaches. The point of the game is to get the ball in the hole in as few strokes as possible. We facilitate that process.** We don't obsess over your faults, but rather we focus on the long-term and lasting impact of your possibilities. You will become a better player by learning how to get out of your own way. And we can help you learn how to do that.

In the pages that follow, you will meet some wildly diverse people who share two things: They love the game of golf, and they have learned to explore that love more fully through our school or books. Oh, yeah, there is a third element they share: They all enjoyed the game more and performed better after

learning the 8 Essentials. The students profiled in this book
include PGA professionals, a touring pro, businessmen and
-women, a dairy farmer from Australia, an F-16 fighter pilot
and an opera singer. They have high handicaps and low, and
they share with you what they learned that has enabled them
to play the game more successfully and enjoy it more completely. Each person's story focuses on a different Essential
Skill, and each chapter ends with exercises you can use—both
on and off the golf course—to help you *Play Your Best Golf
Now*.

Make no mistake about it: We are not anti-instruction, nor
are we anti-analytical. It's just that we believe no component
of the game exists in isolation. It can be just as destructive to
be totally obsessed with swing theory and swing mechanics
as it can be to be obsessed with visualization, strength training or any other piece of the game. We reduce the game to
its simplest, most accessible—and therefore most attainable—
elements, and it is these elements, when combined, that produce great golf.

What results in low scores? Good shots and great putts.
Those good shots and great putts come from swings that
are good enough and putting strokes that are good enough,
which are the result of functional technique. That functional technique is the sum total of your mastery of the
physical, technical, mental, emotional and social elements
of the game, unified within its spirit. Many view golf only
through the micro-lens of technique. We want you to use a

wide-angle lens, seeing all the components that influence your technique.

Have you ever hit a good shot with your swing? Have you ever hit a great shot with your swing? The answer for all of us is yes. **To score, you need to have a good-enough swing and a good-enough putting stroke, but you don't need to be perfect. In fact, the obsession with perfection can be detrimental to performance.** You need to have functional technique, and to maximize the way your technique functions, you need to go one step further and ask this question: What *influences* technique? You'll find the answers in this book; you will learn routines to help you keep your technique performing at its highest level. You will learn to identify what you can control, and you will learn tools that will help you master that control.

There have been many great players throughout the history of golf, and they have had many different swings. Their success comes from the ability to make their swing repeat, especially under pressure. We will help you learn ways to greatly improve the odds of repeatability. The reason we place our emphasis on facilitating your learning, rather than on imposing our teaching, is to help you understand your game better. In that understanding is found sustainable success. That understanding will be with you when we are not. The 8 Essentials will help you get the most out of your relationship with golf, and that leads to lower scores.

What do we mean by getting to know your game better?

The idea is simply to understand that you are more consistent than you think. How are you when you are great? And how are you when you mess up? There are patterns to how you play. **By recognizing these patterns, you can learn to make your confidence less fragile.** You can learn to maximize your performance by getting out of your own way.

When reduced to its basics, golf is a simple game: Get good equipment, make a good swing, and you'll get good results. In recent years, players have also come to realize the value of being in good shape. But many players sense there is something missing from that equation for successful golf. Those who get the most out of their ability seem to possess something others lack, something that seems almost magical.

What is the missing piece of the puzzle? Belief is a huge part of the magic. When Ben Hogan said, "The secret is in the dirt," he meant he played so well under pressure because he had learned to believe in his ability to execute. He had learned how to create confidence. We take the mystery out of the magic and transform implicit knowledge into explicit skills for you. Anyone can have that belief in him or herself.

Many players have come to understand that peak-performance golf involves a whole-game way of looking at the sport. They understand some of the elements that affect scoring but intuitively know there must be others not yet apparent to them. They want to know where to start the search and how to identify the right answers. The answers are in our Essentials. We have drawn you a road map for mastering these

Essentials in order to maximize *your* skills and get the most out of *your* game.

No matter who you are or at what level you play, you need these Essentials to reach your full potential. No matter how often you play, what skill level you possess or what swing theory you believe, you will be better with these Essentials, and you cannot attain your full potential without them. **The 8 Essential Playing Skills are the real deal. They are for every golfer on the planet**. They are derived from an exhaustive understanding of the human experience of playing golf. The 2 Essential Practice Skills will support how you integrate the 8 Essentials into your game.

The Essential Playing Skills stem from all aspects of understanding. Some come from the irrefutable science of the most current research. Others derive from a more intuitive understanding of the game that evolved from our experiences with golf and golfers. Our mission is to transcend swing theories and in that way help all swing theories. We want to support other teachers and enable them to maximize the impact of their instruction by helping them access the Essentials. **The most inspiring thing about the Essentials is that they are available to everyone. They are free. They live inside you**. They do not depend on your skill level. You just have to learn how to bring them out.

The Navajo people have a wonderful phrase to describe an insight that is not brought fully to life: "floating clouds." You can see the vision, you can marvel at its beauty, you can describe its shape and even some of its substance. Then—*poof*—it's gone because you did nothing to transform the vision into reality.

Let there be no more Floating Clouds in your golf game. The 8 Essential Playing Skills are the rope of understanding with which you can lasso your potential. The Essentials available to you in this book can change your game. You will learn routines you can use to get more out of your practice, and you will learn lessons you can take onto the golf course to Play Your Best Golf Now. As you begin your journey with the Essential Playing Skills, ask yourself this: If you had a magic wand, what would you really want from the game? Dream big and make that vision your reality.

CHAPTER 2

Leave Your Mind Behind

"I want to sing like birds sing, not worrying about who hears or what they think."

Rumi, Persian poet and philosopher

SWING KEY: Celebrate the sacred ground of golf.

The cockpit of an F-16 fighter jet is both cramped and complicated, a phone booth–size cocoon of dials and instruments providing endless information, from air speeds that can reach more than 1,600 mph and altitudes as high as fifty thousand feet, to navigational data and information on the mechanical functioning of the plane. One gauge tells the pilot about his target, while another warns him when he has become the target of someone else. To function successfully, the human and the machine must merge as one. This total integration is not an option; it is a necessity.

Trust, and the seamless transition into action that trust allows, is as much the key to executing a perfect F-16 mission as is the mechanical functioning of the plane, the skill of the pilot and the data that goes into the pilot's decision-making. The pilot climbs into the cockpit, is strapped into a harness, hears the disembodied voices of his base and his fellow pilots through his headset, and takes control of the plane. He is a small part of the sophisticated marriage of man and machine, but he is its most important component. **As with any area of human achievement that involves peak-performance activity, success here entails a complicated combination of surrender and control.** You can control how prepared you are; you can control the level of your trust and commitment; and then you have to completely engage with the task that has to be done.

All the clever computer calculations that pour into an F-16 on a combat mission are meaningless without the well-rehearsed actions of the individual at the controls. When the moment of truth arrives, instinct takes over; decisions are not made but rather acted upon. There is no time to think about what you are doing; you must merely do it. This is, literally, a matter of life and death that rests upon the quality of the preparation and the depth of the engagement of the individual. There is no other moment that matters but right now. For success, there can be no doubt in your mind.

This perfect integration of the individual into the action is not a matter of acting without thought, but rather a matter of understanding the task at hand so well that it can be carried out instinctively, without hesitation, reservation or doubt—with complete commitment. Thousands of hours of training and experience translate into the series of split-second judgments, actions and reactions a fighter pilot needs to carry out his mission. **There is, as in all areas of life, a time for thought and a time for action—a time to be in the Think Box and a time to be in the Play Box.** Being in the cockpit of an F-16 fighter jet is all about being in the Play Box.

Every human activity has its Play Box—that moment of truth when you cross the line from thinking about doing something to actually doing it. Whether it is piloting an F-16, performing brain surgery, singing an aria or striking a golf ball, there is one nonnegotiable requirement for achieving the peak-performance state that allows greatness to occur: You have to be 100 percent present through your senses. Most golfers are trained to think while they are performing. But all the research on peak performance shows that to maximize outcome, you need to surrender to the moment and be right here, right now, with all of your senses. Golf is all about those few seconds you spend in the Play Box. Mastery of the Play Box is mastery of golf.

Major Dan Rooney has been an F-16 pilot since enlisting in 1998, and served three tours of duty in Iraq. He is also the founder of Patriot Golf Day, which raises money for the Folds of Honor, a foundation that provides scholarships to the children of servicemen and -women who have been killed or disabled. And he is a PGA of America professional who teaches in Oklahoma and has studied our books. Dan started playing golf when he was five years old with his father, a professor at Oklahoma State University.

"I had four cut-down clubs and a Tony Pena 5-wood, and I was allowed to play with my dad and his friends as long as I didn't fall behind," Dan remembers. "So I'd hit the ball and run, hit the ball and run in the hundred-degree Stillwater, Oklahoma, heat. My dad got the love of the game in me. I told my father when I was twelve that I knew I wanted to be a professional golfer and a fighter pilot. He told me, 'Just find your passion in life and go do that.'"

Dan turned pro right out of the University of Kansas in 1996 and spent a couple years on the mini tours with some success. But he also knew the cutoff age to train to be a fighter pilot was twenty-seven, so he decided that if he didn't get his card at PGA Tour qualifying school late in 1997, he would enlist. "I said to myself that if I didn't make it I would go chase my other dream," says Dan, who majored in sports psychology in college and learned things in the military that prepared him to understand VISION54.

Dan says the concept of the Play Box articulates perfectly what is going on when he is in the cockpit of an F-16—instinct and total engagement with the action take over. While hitting a golf ball pales in importance to flying an F-16 into combat, there are similarities between the state needed to fly a perfect mission and that needed to strike a perfect golf shot. Both are peak-performance activities—or at least should be.

"To be good at flying an F-16 requires extensive preparation and hundreds of hours of training," Dan says. "But once you are in the pilot's seat, being good at it—being great at it—requires that you be one hundred percent present in the cockpit. This incredibly complex activity becomes entirely sensory based. I have a half dozen tasks to carry out with my right hand and just as many to do with my left. If I were thinking about the process instead of being totally engaged in the process, the outcome would be disastrous."

Through our books, Dan came to understand how this experience relates to golf. We know what to do, but when the time comes to execute the swing, we must trust our preparation. This point cannot be emphasized enough: When you cross the Decision Line from the Think Box to the Play Box, the most important things to take with you are trust and commitment. **In the Play Box you must be totally present and through your senses completely engaged with your swing and the shot**. That's where you will find trust. The most important things to leave behind are clutter and doubt, yet that is the baggage most golfers lug with them into the Play Box.

"I have no doubt that if I had flown a fighter first and then played professional golf, I would have had a better chance at making it on tour," Dan says. "Being a fighter pilot is athletic, it involves eye-hand coordination, and everything happens very fast. Both a fighter pilot and a golfer are in the business of the target. When you have troops on the ground—the real heroes—shouting that they need air cover right now, you have to become the calming voice; you have to become the instrument of stability and focus," he explains.

The complexity of piloting an F-16, the pressures of combat and the fact that the lives of others depended on him provided Dan with a foundation upon which to build an expanded vision he applied to golf. "What I learned in flying an F-16 is how to block out distractions. In golf, it is a water hazard or out of bounds. The external stimuli in an F-16 are way more intense than on a golf course. You have to become totally engaged in the process and block out everything else. We have a fear of failure. I'd rather be shot down than mess up."

When you are in the Play Box, you have to be fully engaged in hitting the golf shot at hand. And that is why the first of the 8 Essential Playing Skills for Peak Performance is the concept of the Play Box. This Essential tops your list of priorities. The other seven are of equal importance to one another, but it is through mastering the Play Box skills that peak performance is achieved. This is where golf happens. There are tools you can learn and practice to help you reach that full engagement. Remember, merely understanding the importance of the Play Box is not enough. You have to master a routine for functioning in the Play Box. We can't stress enough the importance of doing the exercises at the end of this chapter and then taking them onto the golf course with you.

We have come to realize that to be successful in the Play Box requires four stages of learning. First, you need to know the difference between thinking and sensing. You can think about dancing, or you can dance. You can think about the correct grip, or you can actually feel it. You don't want to be distracted from the performance by still mentally preparing for the performance while you are in the Play Box. That approach wouldn't work in an F-16, and that approach doesn't work on the golf course. Peak performance is achieved by totally immersing yourself in the experience. Research shows that for peak performance to occur, you need to be in touch with the right side of your brain, where intuition, imagery, perception and heightened sensory awareness reside. The best performers are more left brain in the Think Box and access more of the right brain in the Play Box. You have to learn to make that shift happen. That's getting lost in the moment; that's creating an at-one state that produces great golf shots.

The second stage for a successful Play Box is for you to learn how to stay present with your senses for those precious few seconds you are actually in the Play Box. This takes training. Some players lose their focus as soon as the swing starts. Their mind races into the future and/or it obsesses on some technical thought. Don't let your mind wander! Staying present is challenging but highly achievable. We are not asking you to go to Tibet and meditate for ten years; all we are asking is for you to be fully present to something useful for the few seconds you are in the Play Box.

Third, you need to learn what works best for you to be sensory present in the Play Box. This is a trial-and-error process; explore and discover what works for you. Tiger Woods says that when he's playing his best, he feels the shot in his hands. Annika Sorenstam says she sees the shot, then feels the shot in her stomach and then steps into the Play Box with that feeling and executes. No one can tell you what works best for you in the Play Box. That is your own personal voyage of discovery. The exercises at the end of this chapter will help you figure out what works for you. Find a sensory awareness you can stay present to for the entire swing or stroke, then develop a few options that work for you.

Fourth, how engaged can you be for every shot? To play your best, you have to cultivate the feeling that every shot is the most important shot you will ever hit. Tom Weiskopf once said of Jack Nicklaus: "Jack never hit an indifferent shot in his life." Nicklaus played every shot he ever hit as if it were on the final hole of the U.S. Open. Some players fade in and out of focus during a round; others don't do a good job of conserving energy and lose their Play Box intensity late in the round. You want to have your full focus in your Play Box experience for every shot, not a faded copy. You need to show up for every shot! How do you get good at this concentration? Practice.

When you swim, you don't think about how to swim; when you ride a bike, you don't think about how to ride a bike; and when you walk, your mind is not focused on the mechanics of walking. You swim, you ride, you walk. Make it the same for golf. Don't think—play! One of the players we work with came up with the acronym QDANT to remind herself how she performs her best: Quick, Decisive, Aggressive, No Thoughts. Every Play Box is a brand-new experience beckoning you to show up fully present. Part of what made Nicklaus, Woods and Sorenstam great is that winning never got old for them, playing never got old for them; they were fully engaged with golf all the time and relished the new challenge that comes with every shot.

We want golf to become a sport again. It is not a chess match. It's more like flying an F-16. It should be thrilling. Much golf instruction is about cognitive thinking over the ball—my hands should do this; my legs should do that; etc. That goes against all we know about peak performance. It is virtually impossible to try to hit a golf ball with a "to-do" list in your mind. It would be like trying to go through such a checklist when you are strapped into the cockpit of an F-16 flying at more than the speed of sound. You know what to do—just do it. **The Play Box is where your skill level plus your mental, physical and emotional state—the awareness you bring to the task—equals performance.** You don't bring fear or doubt or hesitancy with you into the Play Box when you dance or swim or ride a bike; don't bring fear or doubt or hesitancy with you when it comes time to hit a golf ball.

"It is all about committing to a process," Dan Rooney says. "The routine in the fighter business is the rock everything is built on. To go through this process and never deviate from the process with all the external stimuli that are going on around you. You have to block out everything except the target and the process. Mentally, as a golfer, I'm a thousand times better than I was. The process is the Think Box and the target is the Play Box."

After your pre-shot routine—the Think Box—you should step into the Play Box committed to your decisions about the shot. In the Play Box, you establish your aim and alignment—you commit to the target—and then perform a committed swing. **The Play Box is about learning the difference between preparing and performing.** The golf swing is not a thought; it is a physical experience. To perform your best, you have to be present through your senses. This is the moment of truth. What do we mean by "be present"? We mean that you are having a first-person experience. You are not concerned about what happens if you miss the putt; you are not calculating what you need to do to shoot your best score; you are not ruminating on that last drive that went left. You are right here, right now. There is only one of you. If you are having a conversation with yourself about anything, that means there are two of you in the Play Box—and neither is focused on hitting the shot.

What do we mean when we say your presence in the Play Box has to be "sensory based"? We mean you are experiencing the task at hand through your senses. Some play their best when they *see* the target in the Play Box, or the trajectory of the ball; others perform better when they *hear* the swing or hum a tune in the Play Box; yet others *feel* a sense of rhythm or tempo while they swing or are more tactile and focus on grip pressure through the swing.

In all cases, you aren't thinking; you are experiencing the shot, you are living the shot. That rich quality of complete engagement cannot be maintained forever. So the less time spent in the Play Box, the better. **We find that for most good players, the Play Box routine lasts between four and nine seconds from the time you step into the shot until you begin the swing.** Taking more time increases the chance that you will distract yourself and that self-talk will start. Taking less time might rush your technique. You also want to keep the Play Box time consistent from the first hole to the last shot of the match. Don't slow down or speed up under pressure. That is a very common occurrence. To be more consistent, you must grasp that being fully engaged for every Play Box is at the heart of consistency.

When you cross that Decision Line into the Play Box, you should feel a sense of liberation, not hesitation. The hard work has been done; the decisions have been made; the practice hours have been recorded. You have committed to the shot. Now comes the fun! It's time to play golf! There is no reason for fear, tension or doubt. Enter the sacred ground and play! We have all experienced that thrilling sensation of a perfectly struck shot. Most players, especially recreational golfers, believe that that state is fleeting. For many, when success happens, there is a part of them that immediately undermines it. That little voice inside is already issuing warnings that the good shots can turn bad at any time.

Peak performance, for most, is a fragile state of confidence. But that does not have to be the case. Peak performance is a state that can be learned and practiced so it can be created more often and last longer. **Confidence doesn't just happen—it is learned. Confidence is under your control.** All those practice swings when you are over the ball are just cramming for the final exam that is the golf shot. Get rid of them! You can't change your skill level in the Play Box, you can't change your level of preparation, but you can be fully present and completely engaged with the shot and target. You can feel better about the shot, and that will lead to a better shot.

How you play is a combination of your skill and your ability to create a peak-performance state. Most golfers practice their skills but leave their mental state up to chance. You need to be competent in both. **Better technique or better conditioning won't help if you can't create a good state for every Play Box on the course. You won't be able to execute.** You can only play with the skills you have. If those skills need to be refined, do it during practice and not in the moment of performance. The Play Box is where you are a performer. You have to be clear about your peak-performance state. Otherwise the Play Box becomes the Hope Box.

Remember when we talked about distinguishing between what you can control and what you can't control? **Being present, being focused—being *there* when it is time to hit a golf shot—is something totally under your control.** To be present, you need to be present *to* something; if not, the Play Box becomes a Nothing Box. Paying attention is a skill you can learn. As we said, you can't go into the Play Box with a checklist of swing thoughts, but it is absurd to think you can go into the Play Box with nothing in your mind. The human brain simply doesn't work that way. **Nature hates a vacuum and immediately tries to fill it.** But you can control what you are paying attention to. You can train yourself to have a quiet mind, and if your mind is not easily quiet, you can train yourself to distract the distracter. You can write the script for your inner monologue.

By staying engaged and busy with your Play Box Awareness your mind is occupied, and nonproductive self-talk fades into the background. Most players need the support of a functional Play Box Awareness; they need something to help turn down the volume of unproductive thoughts. Even players who can create a quiet mind in the Play Box might start hearing the voices under pressure or when they get tired.

They need to learn what to do to get back to the here and now, which is when and where the shot is going to be hit.

If you allow a void to exist in your mind, it will be filled by self-talk, and self-talk is always unproductive, telling you what you can't do or reminding you of how you messed up the last time you were in a similar situation or worrying about the future or trying to remember the last swing tip. To make every Play Box visit an engaging sensory experience, you need to learn tricks—or develop tools, as we like to say—that allow your mind to push aside distractions and focus on hitting the shot. **You need to be proactive; you need to be the one who determines what is going on in your mind when you step into the Play Box.**

While the thought process is left on the other side of the Decision Line, the swing can never go fully on automatic unless you create a situation in which your mind can be free from distraction and doubt. Don't think about what you should be doing; you already know that. But you want to pay attention to something sensory based to allow your body to be free to swing the club. Instead of approaching a shot with trepidation, treat every shot as if you are greeting a long-gone friend returning home—embrace the moment, celebrate it, enjoy it. This is the ability to be totally present.

Your golf experience is an ongoing process. It's not a destination at which you arrive but a road upon which you travel. You must be constantly engaged, from round to round, from hole to hole, from shot to shot. But that does not mean you have to grind yourself down by thinking for five hours. Learn how to take vacations between shots so you save energy for each time you hit a shot. The need to establish the discipline to go in and out of this state of readiness is what makes golf a different and more demanding challenge than most other sports.

Frequently, by the time you get to the fifteenth hole, your play box has lost its shine; it's weak, like a copy of a copy of a copy. The joy that comes from playing golf has gone from a tingly feeling on the first tee to a distracted collection of jumbled thoughts by number fifteen. Your focus is fading. Your Play Box has become passive, not active. **That's why the key to success in the Play Box is to develop your Play Box Awareness.** This is how you stay engaged. This is how you remain constantly integrated with the process of playing golf.

What is Play Box Awareness? It's what you are sensing and experiencing when you step into the Play Box to hit a shot. It could be something you see, feel or hear. Your Play Box Awareness is something that keeps you present and sensory based, the criteria for any peak-performance state. And your Play Box Awareness is something completely under your control.

It is the attention to this Awareness that keeps distracting or negative thoughts out of your head and allows your swing—the swing that has produced great golf shots in the past—to repeat. Play Box Awareness is totally individual-ized. Not only does it vary from person to person, it can vary for you from round to round—sometimes it can even vary within a round. That's why you need a full toolbox of choices.

Perhaps your Awareness takes the form of your concentra-tion on feeling grip pressure, or you count to clear the clutter out of your mind, or you hum a tune. What your Aware-ness is not is a bunch of thoughts about what you should be doing with your swing. You have to find what works for you. The Play Box Awareness is your mantra for success. "Mantra" means "a place to rest the mind." When Yani Tseng won the 2010 Women's British Open at the age of twenty-one, we had her singing songs to herself to keep the self-talk away between shots, and we had her keep her Play Box routine to five seconds so the self-talk wouldn't have time to start up when she was over the ball.

How well you play depends on how successful you are at creating a performance state—a state of total engage-ment—in the Play Box. **The intellect loves to bring stuff into the Play Box. Don't let it. Silence it.** The awareness you take into the Play Box will be something you determine works best for you. When you have found a series of Play Box Awareness choices, they will need to be practiced like any other skill if you want to play your best golf. There is a difference between having a swing awareness in the Play Box and cluttering the Play Box with a to-do list. You might want to feel a certain weight shift in your swing, for example, but that is a physical connection to the swing and not an abstract intellectualization of it.

There are many tools you can use to develop complete engagement in the Play Box. Some seem counterintuitive since they involve bringing thoughts other than golf into the Play Box. But what you are creating is not a to-do list but rather a just-do-it experience. **Think of your Play Box Awareness not as something you have to do but as something that allows you to do what you already know how to do—hit a golf ball.** Remember, great golf is all about creating repeatability, and repeatability of the swing is a physical action. The intellect will always want to get more information. That is the job of the intellect. You have to tame it. More information is not always a good thing. The swing is not an idea—it is an action. Let it flow!

Here are exercises to help you learn what Awareness works best for you in the Play Box. Remember, golf is all about the individual. Experiment, figure out what works for you. Also, remember that knowing the tools is not the same as using them. This is a process with which you must be constantly engaged. No cruise control allowed. Knock knock . . . who's there? You! The shot! The target! Show up!

PLAY BOX EXERCISES

We have found that for most golfers, mastering the Play Box is a step-by-step process, starting with understanding and ending with execution. Here are four steps for mastering your Play Box:

Step 1. Discover the difference between thinking and sensing. In other sports, this happens by itself. The ball comes at you and you catch it. In golf we need to create this performance state since the ball is waiting for us to initiate the action.

- Put a club or a string between the Play Box and the Think Box. Hit ten different shots and make sure you have stopped thinking when you step across the club or string into the Play Box.

- Toss a ball in the air. First think about doing it, then just do it. Next time you eat, think about using your fork for a few bites and then eat without thinking.

- Throw a few balls into a basket. Do this until you sense a freedom of motion. Now step into the Play Box and hit five shots with that physical and mental freedom. Make striking the ball a natural, instinctive act. Repeat one more time. Go to the putting green and do the same for a five-foot putt.

Step 2. Can you pay complete attention to something sensory based the entire time you are in the Play Box? Many golfers need to do Play Box Awareness exercises to learn to pay attention. Learn how to be totally present for the few seconds required to hit a shot.

- Hit three balls, seeing the trajectory in your mind as you swing.

- Hit three balls while humming a tune that makes you happy.

- Hit three balls while feeling a low center of gravity.

- Hit three balls, seeing a spot on the ball.

- Hit three balls, feeling a relaxed jaw.

- Hit three balls while counting or reciting a poem.

- Hit three putts, seeing the line of the putt.

- Hit three putts, listening to the sound of impact.

- Hit three putts, feeling softness in your shoulders.

- Hit three pitch shots, seeing a bright orange landing spot in your mind as you swing.

- Hit three pitch shots, listening to the silence inside your head as you swing.

- Hit three shots, feeling the tension level in your arms as you swing.

How well could you stay focused with the awareness? Was it easier with some shots than others? Take notes about what works and what doesn't work for you to pay full attention in the Play Box. This is practicing being present.

Step 3. What sensory awareness allows you to be most engaged with the shot? Is it visual, auditory, tactile or a combination? The only way you will find out is to start exploring.

- Hit three shots, seeing the ball flight in your mind's eye.

- Hit three shots, feeling the grip pressure.

- Hit three shots, listening to the impact. For the first three assignments, do the same in chipping and pitching.

- Hit three putts, seeing the ball fall into the cup in your mind's eye.

- Hit three putts, feeling a low center of gravity.

- Hit three putts while singing or humming aloud.

- Hit three shots, counting backward during your swing.

- Hit three shots, feeling your feet.

- Hit three shots, seeing a green neon line moving to the target and back to your ball.

Write down three Play Box Awareness choices that work best for you. Are they visual, auditory, tactile/kinesthetic or a combination? Is it the same for full shots, short-game shots and putts? This is a starting template, so keep being creative with more choices for your Play Box!

Step 4. How fully engaged can you be in the Play Box? If you are not near to 100 percent engaged on every shot, you are greatly diminishing your chances of hitting good shots.

Explore how much time is best for you to spend in the Play Box to remain fully engaged.

- How many consecutive shots can you hit being 100 percent engaged in the Play Box?

- Hit three shots with a three-second Play Box routine.

- Hit three shots with a six-second Play Box routine.

- Hit three shots with a nine-second Play Box routine.

- Play nine holes with only a Play Box routine and no Think Box routine. Pick the target and use your instincts to decide what club to hit and what shot to play. What is that like?

Go on the golf course and choose a Play Box Awareness and notice how well you stay committed to it. How does your level of engagement vary from shot to shot and from hole to hole? It's vital to take practice onto the course. Rate yourself on your level of commitment to each Play Box.

You are a Play Box Master when:

- You are 100 percent present for every Play Box on the golf course.

- You have identified several choices for your best Play Box Awareness.

- You have the skill and discipline to be engaged for the entire Play Box.

- You are consistent with the time you spend in the Play

Box on the course, and the time you spend in the Play Box is with full engagement.

Functional Play Box: You can separate thinking from sensing, and you know what to sense in the Play Box.

Masterful Play Box: For eighteen holes, you are able to be 100 percent present in the Play Box for every shot.

CHAPTER 3

Decide and Commit

"Some persons are very decisive when it comes to avoiding decisions."

Brendan Francis, Irish author

SWING KEY: The perfect golf shot begins with a clear and congruent decision and a full commitment to that decision.

Unlike frequently traveled highways, turning points in life are rarely heralded by road signs. At best, they are a fleeting glimpse in the rearview mirror, recognized only after you fully experience and recognize the importance of the change in direction. The right path is often less a landmark beckoning to you than it is a feeling whispering to you. Sometimes, the smartest thing you can do is to listen.

Such was the case for Marlo Stil, an investment advisor who made not only a midlife career change but, through golf and our school, discovered a whole new path and passion. When Marlo found golf, it was like turning the corner of a city block and running into a total stranger who becomes your best friend. When she found VISION54, it led her to an understanding of the game, through which she realized that the new friend stumbled upon was actually the love of her life.

When Marlo decided to leave her corporate job and work for herself, she was able to create more time for golf. Soon after reinventing herself, Marlo used hard work and lots of practice to get her handicap down to 14—and then in 2002 she came to one of our programs, the first of many she has attended. Within a year, she had her handicap down to 2. How can such startling improvement be possible?

Part of Marlo's breakthrough as a golfer was the realization that great shots are born in belief. For Marlo, Decide and Commit was the Essential Playing Skill that had the most impact on her game. The ability to make a clear decision and commit to it is an activity that takes place in the Think Box, but the nature of this routine for *you* is determined by *your* particular needs in the Play Box. The ability to decide and commit in the Think Box frees you to perform in the Play Box.

The Play Box is golf, while the Think Box is the dress rehearsal for golf. We have come to realize the importance of developing a Think Box routine that gets you to the Play Box quickly in a confident and committed state of mind. This is a case where working backward is the most forward-looking approach. The key to developing a good Think Box routine lies in understanding what preconditions you need to achieve peak performance once you are in the Play Box.

The Think Box has two elements. The first is to figure out what you need to do to make it easier to be in the right state to swing at your best when you step into the Play Box. For some, this means making practice swings to feel the shot; for others, it involves visualizing the shots; still others need to exhale and calm down; while yet others need to find a way to amp up before crossing the Decision Line.

The second Think Box element is to make a clear, informed decision about the shot. That is what this chapter is about: **You need to learn how to make a decision and commit to that decision—and this is a learned skill.** We find that too many players spend too much time in the Think Box, delaying the real activity of golf—hitting the shot. When you leave the Think Box and step into the Play Box, you have to be completely committed to the decision you have made about the shot you are about to hit. Get the facts you need (yardage, etc.), then decide on a strategy for the shot based on an honest evaluation of your ability and the level of trust you have at that moment. That commitment to your decision is all you need to find in the Think Box.

One of the great things about sports is that they speed up the clock of human existence. You can learn a lot about yourself, or someone else, in an extremely compressed period of time by playing games. In a round of golf, you can learn how you handle failure or success and how you deal with disappointment or bad luck. And you learn to what extent you are willing to formulate a plan and commit to that plan. Part of what Marlo learned was that she needed a greater resolve to carry total commitment into the Play Box. "Through VISION54, I have learned the power of putting complete attention on my intentions," says Marlo. **"I have also learned the importance—the necessity, really—of making clear, complete and congruent decisions."** When Marlo started to do that, her scores began to drop.

One of the keys to being able to Decide and Commit is making your Think Box routine efficient. Simplify your routine to the basics of what you need to prepare for a shot. This varies from person to person. Some people play based on total instinct, and the Think Box is not an Essential for them. They look at the shot, commit to a decision, and step up and hit the ball. Some players we have worked with found it liberating when they reduced their thinking and just focused on being committed in the Play Box. **Overthinking can lock you up both mentally and physically.** Unfortunately, the overintellectualization of the game has led many to believe that slowing down is being careful when, in fact, it is being careless.

So let's talk about the decision-making process. Every shot demands that you make multiple decisions: about your club, your target, the wind, the lie, your strategy, etc. Then you have to learn to commit to those decisions. There is no way to know in advance if you are making the right decision, but you still have to commit to that decision. Evaluate the shot *after* you hit it; don't worry about the outcome *before* you hit it. When Tiger Woods was struggling in 2010 after he switched coaches—and was trying to change his swing—he was asked to explain why the new swing worked sometimes and not other times, and he gave a one-word answer: "Commitment." The full commitment wasn't always there.

Not every decision works out and not every shot is struck solidly, but the more committed you are to your decision, the better your misses will be. And as six-time major champion Nick Faldo once said: "Golf is not about the quality of your good shots; it is about the quality of your bad shots." Faldo was excellent at commitment, and one of his great strengths as a player was that his bad shots were never far off. He consistently beat players more physically talented than he was.

The trust that you develop in your decisions is a product of both your head and your heart. Your plan, the decision, is mostly the job of the head. Then you have to decide to jump on board and commit—that's the job of the heart. While Decision and Commitment come from the intellect, they should also be intuitive and instinctual. Don't make this Essential merely a mechanical recording of yardage and wind direction. Feel your belief. Breathe your confidence.

The decision-making process involves *what* you say to yourself and *how* you say it. Some people need very little information to make their decision, while others need precise yardages, practice swings and caddie talk. Again, figure out what works best for you. The research shows that many golfers take in too much information, and by the time they enter the Play Box, they have no energy for the shot and their performance is undermined by confusion.

The greatest decision makers in any activity get a baseline of information and then listen to their instincts. How do you know what is good for you? Figure out what is absolutely essential for you in the decision-making process and what is optional. Try playing with minimal or no information and gradually add more information until you have everything possible. Where on that spectrum do you perform the best—bare bones or jam-packed?

We want you to be who you are on the golf course, not a programmed robot trying to be someone else. If you know you play your best by making mostly gut decisions, then do that. Players like this frequently just say, "I got it," when asked about their decision about the shot. Then there are those who need more time before a shot, which can either be external—measuring yardage, wind, etc.—or internal—a vision of the swing they want to make. Remember, it is you finding what works for you. For many players, decisions are a combination of inner awareness and an outer connection to the target.

Now that you have decided about the shot, how do you communicate that decision to yourself? This is a crucial step. This is how you develop trust for the shot. Try using a video camera so you can see how you look during the decision process. How is your body language? How are your eyes? Watch tape of great players like Jack Nicklaus or Annika Sorenstam. Their level of commitment to their decisions almost screams at you in their body language and facial expressions. They believed in what they were doing. Tom Lehman once said that Seve Ballesteros played with a body language that shouted, "This next shot is going to be the greatest shot you have ever seen."

Great players have a positive voice in their head; so should you. Here is the kind of conversation you might have with yourself: "The pin is on the back-right part of the green and it is one hundred and sixty yards away. I am going to hit a 6-iron with a left-to-right ball flight so my target is the tall tree behind the left-center of the green, and I will swing with eighty percent of my normal tempo. The ball will start out on a line for that tree and then fade to where the hole is located."

Notice that you do not say, "I *think* it is a 6-iron" or "I am going to *try* to cut it" or "I *hope* it will fade to where the hole is." Clear. Concise. Positive. Know what you want to do with the shot and trust that you are going to do it. In our school, we pair off students, and when they play, we have them actually say to each other what their intention is for every shot they hit. For many players, verbalizing their intentions for the shot amplifies the commitment to the shot.

Try this: For several shots, say out loud what you would normally say to yourself. Is your voice clear and congruent or are you using vague words like "try" or "maybe" or "think" or "hope"? The chances of executing your decision successfully are greatly increased if you have communicated that decision to yourself with clarity and certainty.

Several years ago we had a woman at our school whose technical skills were a lot better than her handicap. After seeing her on the golf course, we realized one of the main reasons for this discrepancy was her inability to make congruent decisions. We had her do an exercise in which she would say her decisions about the shot aloud before stepping into the Play Box. Her voice, her body language and her words were extremely tentative and weak. She would say: "I will try to hit it over the hill, but I don't like this hole and I have never played this hole well."

Lynn challenged her by saying: "Come on now, get clear and tell me, tell yourself and tell everyone else here what you want to do with the shot in a way that we will believe you." The straw hat the woman had been wearing came flying off, and she pointed her finger and said in a strong voice: "OK, this is what I'm going to do: I'll aim at the tree behind the green and swing with confidence to the finish." She then proceeded to hit her best shot ever on the hole, and proceeded to stay with that commitment the rest of the round. About two months later, she told us her game had turned around, her handicap had dropped, and she was enjoying golf more. She thanked us for the "scream therapy." She had learned how to develop clear, confident decisions.

Three younger men playing mini-tour golf came to us for coaching. They had great swings but were not happy with how they performed in competition. We started checking their VISION54 performance foundations, and early on became suspicious of their commitment level on the course. We suggested that at the next tournament they put a check mark on the scorecard each time they committed to a decision on the course. All three of them averaged being fully committed on only about 40 percent of their shots. Should they be working on their mechanics or should they be working on improving the percentage of shots to which they were fully committed? Improve the commitment and the technique will get better! A great swing with a tentative hope in the Play Box does not lead to great golf shots.

One interesting observation we have made is that different ways of speaking to yourself work for different people. For example, you could say: "I will hit a high shot landing ten feet short of the hole." That works for some, but others feel like they are being told what to do, and don't respond well to that direction. If you ask yourself the question, "Will I hit a high shot, landing ten feet short of the hole?" that requires you to internally answer the question and own that answer before stepping into the shot. That approach works for others.

Annika Sorenstam was one of the best in the history of golf at making decisions and then having the courage to carry them out. But this was not an easy thing for her to learn.

Early in her career, Annika would write on her visor, "Face your fear," as a reminder of the commitment she needed to carry with her into the Play Box. Ai Miyazato started to win LPGA tournaments when she found a similar level of belief in her decisions. You can literally talk yourself into being a better player.

On the final hole of the 2009 Samsung World Championship, Ai was leading by one stroke over Na Yeon Choi. With 205 yards left to a green guarded by water and with a so-so lie, Ai decided to hit a 5-wood instead of laying up. The ball landed on the front of the green and rolled back into the water, and Ai finished second by one stroke. We were very curious as to how she was going to handle this disappointing outcome.

When we saw her, the first thing Ai said was, "It was a five," and she didn't mean a 5-wood. Ai had been training herself to fully commit to her decisions. She rates herself after shots on a scale of one to five, with five meaning complete commitment to the shot. "I knew the distance and the lie, and felt that I could totally trust going for it," she said. "I want to practice being an aggressive player in these situations, and since I didn't know how Na Yeon would play the hole, being a hole behind me, I went for it." Ai left the tournament not with disappointment, but with a feeling of mastering the skill of Decision and Commitment. She knew this skill would lead to future victories.

The second LPGA event of the 2010 season was played

in Singapore. Ai was once again leading by one stroke going into the final hole. After a great drive, she discussed the club selection with her caddie, who gave her the yardage and said he thought it was a 6-iron. But Ai's gut told her it was a 5-iron. No one else except the player hitting the shot can know what is going on inside of that player. Ai took the 5-iron and with full commitment hit it twelve feet left of the hole and won the tournament.

When making shot decisions, it is crucial that you be honest with yourself. In the 1993 Masters, Chip Beck came to the par-5 fifteenth hole at Augusta National three strokes behind Bernhard Langer. Beck had 236 yards to carry the water in front of the green, and the shot was playing into a slight breeze. A massive gallery lined the fairway and surrounded the green, and millions more were watching on TV. An eagle 3 would get Beck right back in the hunt. The tension level was enormous.

After careful consideration, Beck reached into his bag, pulled out a 5-iron and lay up short of the water, thinking he could hit a wedge close with his third shot, make a birdie and pick up one stroke without the risk of hitting the ball into the water and losing all chance at victory. A murmur of surprise rippled through the gallery. On TV, a measure of disbelief was expressed. Why was Beck not being more aggressive in such a do-or-die situation?

Unfortunately, Beck ended up making par on the hole, because he hit a poor third shot, and ultimately finished in second place, four strokes behind Langer. For years, Beck has been second-guessed about laying up when he had a chance to win the Masters. And for years, he's defended his shot selection. "I didn't want to throw away my chances to win, and that shot would have been stupid," Beck explained.

Shortly after the Masters, Byron Nelson, one of the great players and great gentlemen of the game, was asked about Chip's decision. "I would never second-guess another man in a situation like that," Nelson said. "Maybe the shot didn't fit his eye. Maybe he wasn't comfortable with the lie. Maybe he wasn't sure he could pull it off. Only he knows what he is feeling."

Nelson raises great points about the process that goes into making Decision and Commitment judgments. Beck never explained the shot in a broader context than simple strategy—he could make birdie by laying up and not risk the penalty stroke of going into the water—and left unsaid was the clear implication that he did not completely believe in his ability to pull off the shot. In that regard, he made the proper decision.

This is a crucial point. **The decision you commit to should take into consideration your state in the Play Box.** How have you been hitting the ball today? What is your energy level like for the challenges of this shot? How are you handling the pressure of the situation right now in your match? This is a time to be totally honest with yourself. To do otherwise is denial and courting disaster.

You must have a well-grounded knowledge of your game and your ability. That's a difficult task for many players. Most recreational players make their shot selection based on their best shot, not their average shot. Honesty under pressure is a valuable commodity. In that regard, Chip Beck probably did the right thing in laying up at that time. But if Beck had possessed a broader range of skills to use in pressure situations like that, he might have reached the decision that this was the time to go for the green, and he might have been able to commit to that decision with the complete confidence he could pull off the shot.

"Confidence must be practiced," says Marlo Stil. "And it is best practiced under the specific circumstances and conditions where it will be needed. My confidence is built through trust, and trust in myself is gained by keeping committed to working on things I can control that will help me be a better player down the road."

When we work with players, we hardly ever add to their Think Box routine. Mostly, we take things out and try to simplify the process. Players who overanalyze their shot options and endlessly rehearse their swing are less committed to their decisions and less satisfied with the results. Remember, as with all aspects of the game, everything you do in the Think Box should have a purpose, and that purpose is to get ready for the Play Box. Eliminate pointless actions. That will also make your playing partners happy as your pace of play improves!

A lot of the learning that goes on at our school happens away from the range or the golf course, often in relaxed conversation. One of the questions we like to ask to get our players thinking is this: If five frogs are on a lily pad and one decides to jump into the water, how many frogs are left? Most people say four, but the answer is five. Because the frog decided to jump doesn't mean he jumped. He might not have been committed to his decision.

Commitment is not a teeth-grinding, muscle-up experience. You can be fully committed and still do something very soft with a shot. It's all about fully trusting the decision you have made and putting it into action. You can train trust and your ability to face up to the shot. The best place to practice this skill is on the golf course. That's where the lily pads are. Put a mark on the scorecard for each shot you hit with 100 percent commitment. No matter what your handicap is, you can learn to master this skill. Decide. Commit. Jump!

DECIDE AND COMMIT EXERCISES

1. Decision-making practice

- Hit shots on the practice area or on the golf course and say your decision about the shot aloud before stepping into the Play Box. What do you say and how do you say it?

- While on the course or on the practice area, experiment with minimizing the amount of information you need before the shot. Start by looking at the target and intuitively choosing a club before hitting your shot, without checking the yardage. Begin again, and add more information before making the decision. Try this numerous times on a scale of one to four, with one being acting only on instinct and four being a flood of information. Do this a few times. What amount of information between one and four allows you to execute the best in the Play Box?

- Hit six putts from a distance of fifteen feet. Change your preparation level for each. On the first putt, play like a kid and do nothing in preparation. For each subsequent putt, add some more preparation. On the sixth putt, check everything. No stones unturned! Where in that spectrum did you putt the best?

- Hit ten different putts from fifteen feet. For each putt before stepping over the Decision Line, imagine in vivid detail how the ball will roll into the cup.

- Hit shots where you alternate between stating your decision with a weak and indecisive voice and body language, and doing it as if you were the most confident player in the world. What is the difference for you?

2. Commitment practice

- Check your level of commitment. Physically create a separation between the Think Box and the Play Box by placing a string or a club on the ground behind the ball. Hit ten shots with different clubs, doing your full routine. What are you feeling when you cross this

Decision Line from the Think Box into the Play Box? What percentage of shots did you hit while fully committed? Do the same on the putting green.

- For a full practice session on the range, short-game area and putting green, only hit shots when you are fully committed. If you feel any hesitation, step back across the line and reload. How often did you need to step back? Commitment is a skill that needs to be trained and maintained.

- Hit ten consecutive shots with full commitment. If any of the shots has less than 100 percent commitment, start over. Mix it up with different types of shots. Do your complete routine.

- Hit twelve consecutive putts where your commitment to the decision is 100 percent.

- Hit three different tricky chip shots, three different tricky pitch shots, and three different tricky bunker shots. Did you have full commitment for each shot?

3. Decide and Commit practice

- Hit shots on the range with a friend. Have the friend pick the target and tell you what kind of shot to hit. It could be a 5-iron low draw to a one-hundred-yard marker. How committed did you stay to the decision? Do this ten times, then make your own decisions and commit to them for another ten shots.

- Keep track of how well you commit to your decisions for each shot during a round. On what percentage of the shots did you fully commit?

Functional Decide and Commit: You can commit fully to your decision for ten shots in a row on the course.

Masterful Decide and Commit: For eighteen holes you are 100 percent fully committed to your decision for every shot.

CHAPTER 4

Find Your Balance

"Happiness is not a matter of intensity but of balance,
order, rhythm and harmony."

Thomas Merton, American Trappist monk

SWING KEY: The perfect shot is not merely a physical
act, but a human act.

Have you ever watched a figure skater stick a triple
jump, or a gymnast race across the mat and twirl
high into the air before returning to her feet in perfect balance? When those incredibly skilled, complicated and
athletic acts are flawlessly performed, it is usually within the
rhythm created by movement. Quite literally, these athletes
have a running start at greatness. This is a head start toward
peak performance that golfers don't have—unless they have
the tools of the Essential Playing Skills.

One of the challenges of the golf swing is that this graceful motion begins from a completely still, static position.

There is no running start. The tension and the doubt that are often consumed by movement in other sports can creep into the body and mind of a golfer more easily because there is so much "downtime" in the game. This is why it is essential for you to build a bridge between yourself and your skills—a bridge that will take you into the Play Box in a peak-performance state, committed and without fear or doubt. This is also why many players have better balance if they do some kind of a waggle or keep in motion as they address the ball, instead of getting too static. The waggle is the transition from stillness to motion.

This transition from address to the swing is challenging. Think of walking from bright sunlight into a dark room. Eventually, your eyes do adjust and you function perfectly in your new environment. But the transition does not come without some initial difficulty in seeing. The same is true when you leave that dark room and return to the sunlight. The real challenges of life are not when you are in the room but rather when you make entrances and exits.

Golf is a series of entrances and exits. The swing is the room. The pre-shot routine is the entrance and the post-shot routine is the exit. The goal is to start completely centered and balanced, execute the swing, and then return to being completely centered and balanced. From sunlight to darkness and back to sunlight without tripping! This is an easily disrupted process that requires not just technique but understanding.

In the next three chapters, we are going to discuss the three Essentials that define your swing, the Essentials that make your swing your signature on the golf course. **These Essentials are Balance, Tempo and Tension Awareness.** The only way for you to completely integrate your physical and technical skills into an efficient golf swing is by finding your balance, feeling the tempo that works for you and recognizing where your tension resides, and developing strategies for dealing with that tension.

Again, to go back to our darkened room metaphor: Experience allows you to develop strategies for dealing with the transition. You learn to take it slowly after making your entrance or exit, until your eyes adjust. Our experience working with golfers has led us to understand the importance of Balance, Tempo and Tension Awareness. That experience has also led us to develop tools to help you enter the Play Box in a calm, rhythmic, balanced state and exit it the same way.

We have met very few players in our work who have as much passion for the game of golf as Walter Owen, or Topper, as his friends call him. A businessman from Southern California, Topper had been playing the game for more than a half century when he came to us after reading about VISION54 in *The Wall Street Journal*. Topper approached us at a time when his passion for the game was being challenged.

"I was struggling with mental and emotional habits on the course that were leaving me unaware of the physical reality and the technical truth that would allow me to create the shots that are possible in the situation at hand," Topper says. These bad habits disrupted his technique, "leading to some nasty yips, shanks and other assorted clobbered shots that would challenge anyone's self-image as a player," he says. He was in a downward spiral.

As his handicap rose from +2 to 4, Topper instinctively understood that his problems existed not because he had all of a sudden forgotten how to play golf or because his technique had drastically deteriorated, but rather because something was interfering with his execution of the swing and putting stroke. He just didn't know how to approach the problem. The more he struggled, the less fun he had, and the less fun he had, the more he struggled.

Fortunately, Topper avoided one of the biggest mistakes many golfers make. Players of every skill level, when they are struggling, start tinkering with their swing. Some even embark on the dangerous path of trying to change their swing. They assume that when their game leaves them—and everyone goes into a slump at some point—the reason for the poor play is always a mechanical issue. Such a drastic action as a swing change should always be the last resort.

Of course, when we don't play well, it is because our technique falters. But the real question is why the technique faltered. Where did the problem originate? If you don't commit to a decision, it shows up in the technique. If you are cluttered with swing thoughts in the Play Box, it shows up in the technique. If you have too much adrenaline, it might affect your tempo and show up in the technique. At times it is something mechanical, like faulty alignment or misplaced ball position in the stance, but very often the technique problem is just a symptom of another problem.

Swing changes are difficult even for the most gifted athletes, and often the problems that exist do not require blowing up your swing and starting all over, but rather fine-tuning what you have. **Before you start tinkering with your swing—which always makes you worse before you get better—check your BTT: Your *Balance*, *Tempo* and *Tension Awareness*.** Trust us on this: It will only make you better. Attention to your BTT can never be overdone. BTT improves your swing without you consciously changing your swing! These elements are essential to a solid physical swing.

The concept of BTT was a crucial breakthrough for Topper. "The comprehensive, holistic approach of VISION54 is fundamental for me, and perhaps all, to dig out the bad habits and cultivate the ones required for golf glory and in finding your game," he says. "It is a great privilege to be so schooled by the great game, which humbles as harshly as nature's indifference to human folly."

In our program, Topper came to understand that his game was simply out of balance. He had become an angry player and as a result had lost his balance on the golf course. While there are many different kinds of golf swings that function successfully, they all have these three things in common: The player is in *Balance*, he has found the *Tempo* that works for him, and he has established a *Tension Awareness* that allows him to repeat his swing—especially under pressure.

"I shot 69 today with *lots* of shots left to be had," Topper wrote to us after he had been at our school. "Putting was unproductive. I missed seven inside fifteen feet and left a little bunker shot in the bunker. I have benefited greatly from Play Box involvement with balance. BTT is the platform on which the mechanics manifest. Now I can experience my mechanics instead of intending them, which was so often untoward."

If you focus on BTT, as Topper did, work to develop the tools we have designed for BTT improvement and take them with you into the Play Box, you will see the results in the way you perform. You will shoot lower scores. One of the keys to improving your game is determining what area of focus in your practice will yield the most results. If there were one thing you could work on that would have the greatest impact in making you a better player, what would it be?

For many players, the single biggest improvement factor is working on their BTT. If you are coming over the top, perhaps the flaw is not in your swing but rather in your balance or tempo or a result of tension. Those great shots you hit are not accidents but rather the result of smooth execution. That silky execution comes at those times when you make a swing in balance, at your ideal tempo and without tension. You can make that happen more often. The golf swing is a graceful, balletlike movement that is most effective when it finds its own rhythm.

We will start in this chapter with *Balance*. No matter what swing you have, if you make that swing in better balance, you will get better—and more consistent—results. **You cannot make a golf swing that your body cannot execute.** That's just a simple fact. The key is to find the swing that works for you—your one, true golf swing—and then develop the tools that enable you to repeat that swing. Being in balance is your running start to greatness.

Simply put, the physical foundation of your golf swing is balance. Think of your swing like a toy top set in motion by the pulling of a string. The top is most graceful in its movements when it is totally centered, in complete balance. As it slows down, that balance is lost and it starts to wobble. Eventually it topples over and the string must be pulled again. That process is like making the golf swing over and over.

The goal is to find that balance. And a key understanding is that you can always return to that balance even when you have lost it. You can always pull the string and set the top back in motion. Remember, focus on what you can control and ignore what you can't control. This is critical mental triage. You can't control your score, but you can control many of the things that contribute to your score, and establishing and maintaining balance is definitely within your control.

"Physical balance is crucial," says Topper. "Poised, pinpoint balance naturally and automatically contributes to even, steady tempo, allowing your core body rotation to carry the hands smoothly on their path. Precise balance allows you to move with an unhurried and focused feeling. Balance is a meta-fundamental that can be exploited to great advantage."

Think of that feeling when you hit a perfect shot. It is almost as if time stands still. Everything flows together as one for you. **Whether the perfect shot is produced by the long, fluid swing of Sam Snead or by the eye-blink quick one of Ben Hogan, balance is maintained throughout.** For many of the players we work with, one of the most important aspects of their warm-up routine is nurturing balance. Smart players realize they are not going to change anything on the warm-up tee, but they can find something: balance.

Balance is like fresh produce: It can go bad very easily. It also changes from day to day. You should practice in order to access and maintain a good baseline level of balance. We are dynamic, changing human beings, and we will swing well more often if we do regular balance exercises as maintenance. Many players practice balance by standing on one foot or using different balance tools at the gym.

For the sake of your golf, it's very important that you are able to transfer stationary balance to rotational balance. That is what you need for your golf swing. We see many players who are able to stand on one leg with their eyes closed for thirty seconds, but then when we ask them to rotate at the same time, they fall over right away. When you make the golf swing, your body must rotate. You must be able to maintain balance not just when you are stationary, but when you are in motion as well. The swing is a dynamic action.

If you can step onto the first tee with a sense that you are centered like that spinning top, you will bring a calm with you into the Play Box that will greatly increase your chances of repeatedly making great swings. And you do not have to let that balance be a hope thing, but rather it can be a sure thing. You can make it happen; this is one of the things under your control.

A key first step is to realize that balance can be disrupted by a wide variety of things and that these disruptive factors vary from person to person. **What throws your game out of balance?** Anger? Fear? Not warming up properly? Not having a Playing Focus to engage your mind? Not eating right? The simple fact that you are out of sorts on this particular day? The first key to maintaining your balance is to understand yourself.

Anytime we think too much and all our energy is up in our head, it affects our balance. We all remember the way Tiger Woods struggled in 2010 after difficulties in his personal life became public. Even someone as talented and mentally focused as Tiger is vulnerable to the delicate nature of balance. He was distracted. And what is the mental image you have of Tiger when he hits a wild shot? He ends up out of balance, often dropping his club or letting go with one hand.

Yes, Woods had swing issues in 2010, but those issues were magnified by the fact that he wasn't completely engaged in the process of playing golf. That was shown by his erratic short game, which had nothing to do with the head dip in his swing but rather with the dip in his concentration level. Tiger had lost his balance, he had lost his way.

To some degree, this happens to all of us. The balance of the swing is a physical thing wedded to our mental and emotional state. "Emotional realities drive the physical bus," Topper says. "Running off the track is a physical manifestation, but the driver must be considered, especially when the emotion rises. Getting through to the truth and meaning of how you feel emotionally is utterly key to realizing the athletic functioning required to swing the golf club properly."

Topper had become an angry player and was not even aware of it. That led to his becoming an unhappy player. And there is no way you can play your best golf in that state. When Topper realized this and learned some of our tools to maintain his emotional balance, he dropped his handicap to 0.2 and said, "My ambition is to get it lower still." He is back in balance on the golf course in every sense of the word.

One of the questions we like to ask players is this: "If you had only five minutes to warm up for your round, what single thing could you work on that would have the greatest impact on how you play?" For Topper, it is definitely balance. And by doing some simple exercises that focus on physical balance, he is improving his mental balance by taking control of the situation and doing everything within his control to get ready for the round of golf ahead. Working on his physical balance strengthened his mental belief in his ability to perform.

Some of the exercises we give you below may take you out of your comfort zone, and some of them may get you some odd looks on the practice range. Don't let that inhibit you. These work. They are part of the great assortment of tools we have developed to help you stay in balance and regain your balance when you lose it. Many are also tools you can take onto the course with you.

BALANCE EXERCISES

- Hit five shots with your feet together.
- Hit five shots, standing on your right foot.
- Hit five shots, standing on your left foot.
- Hit five shots with your eyes closed.
- Hit five shots using only your left arm and standing on your right foot.
- Hit five shots using only your right arm and standing on your left foot.
- Hit five shots barefooted.
- Hit five shots, standing on your left toes.
- Hit five shots, standing on your right toes.

Do each exercise with a variety of clubs and see how many swings you can finish in balance. If it is difficult, start with small swings and a slower tempo. Pick the exercises that match your skill level, and as you get better, move on to the others.

- Hit a chip shot standing on your right foot and using your left arm. Alternate by standing on your left foot and swinging with your right arm. Do this five times.

- Hit putts alternating between standing on the right foot only, left foot only, on the toes of the right foot, on the toes of the left foot, and eyes closed and feeling a low center of gravity.

- Hit ten consecutive bunker shots in which you finish with your weight on your front foot. Vary each shot to different targets.

- Hit five shots left-handed if you are a right-handed player, and right-handed if you are a left-handed player. Do it with a 7-iron turned around. Do the same on the chipping green.

- Juggle with three golf balls for four minutes.

Functional Balance: You are able to hit ten consecutive shots with your feet together, five on only the left foot, and five on only the right foot, all finishing in balance.

Masterful Balance: You can hit ten consecutive shots with your feet together, ten on your right foot only, ten on your left foot only, five with your eyes closed, five standing on the toes of your right foot, and five standing on the toes of your left foot, all finishing in balance.

CHAPTER 5

Feel Your Tempo,
Dance to Its Rhythm

"The tempo is the suitcase. If the suitcase is too small, everything is completely wrinkled. If the tempo is too fast, everything becomes so scrambled you can't understand it."

Daniel Barenboim, conductor and pianist

 SWING KEY: Find the tempo that works for you in the chaos surrounding you.

St. Andrews is a tiny university town of somber stone buildings that clings to the east coast of Scotland with a fierceness that mirrors the pride of the people who created and have defended a culture there for more than a thousand years. Of the many roles the Old Grey Toon plays in history, none surpasses its place in golf. While there may be disagreement as to where the first golf ball was struck, there is no doubt that St. Andrews is where the game was formalized.

The first rules were written there in 1754, three centuries after King James II banned golf because it distracted men from archery practice, a skill needed to defend the kingdom. Without dispute, the Old Course at St. Andrews is the Home of Golf.

So it was that the 2007 Ricoh Women's British Open was a celebration. For the first time, women professionals would compete on the Old Course and have access to the clubhouse of the male-only Royal & Ancient Golf Club. The streets of St. Andrews were packed that week. Tables at restaurants were difficult to find, and making your way to the bar to get a pint at the Dunvegan Hotel took a wee bit of work.

The pros virtually floated above the cobblestones, made weightless by the thrill of participating in history. Everyone wanted to be the first woman to win at St. Andrews, a place where Mary Queen of Scots was said to have played golf in the 1500s. Among the star-studded field was twenty-two year-old Ai Miyazato, who had already won more than a dozen tournaments in her native Japan but was looking for her first triumph on the LPGA Tour.

Miyazato had joined the LPGA a year earlier, arriving in America accompanied not only by the high hopes of her country, but also by a media contingent numbering in the dozens that reported on her every round—virtually on her every shot. The expectations were that Ai would conquer America just as she had Japan. But while aspiration provides the vision upon which the road map for success is drawn, unreasonable expectations can saddle the individual with excess emotional baggage that bogs down the journey.

Miyazato had, by any reasonable measuring stick, a very successful rookie LPGA season in 2006, finishing number twenty-two on the season-ending money list. But more was expected. The question began to be whispered: "What's wrong with Ai?" More disturbingly, some began to question whether she was good enough to ever win an LPGA tournament. The tempo of Ai's game—of her life—had been thrown out of whack by external forces.

By the time Miyazato got to St. Andrews, she was midway through another winless season, but was feeling good about her game. She had high hopes, especially after an opening-round 70 left her just three strokes off the lead. Then eighteen months of pressure came crashing down upon her. An 80 in the second round followed by 77 and 79 on the weekend caused Ai to tumble to a tie for fifty-eighth place. She left St. Andrews in tears, breaking down during questioning by the Japanese media. A downward spiral began in which she would fail to finish her next five tournaments and finish fifty-seventh or worse seven times in her next eight starts.

During that difficult week at St. Andrews, Ai's father, Masuru Miyazato, who had quite successfully coached Ai and her two brothers, both also professionals, asked if we would formally get involved in Ai's coaching. She knew about VISION54. In fact, Ai wrote the foreword to the Japanese version of *Every Shot Must Have a Purpose*, our first book. We had been watching her for some time, and we knew that the technical problems she was having were tied to the pressure on her to win.

One trademark of Ai's game is her smooth, consistent tempo. We have seen people literally gasp in admiration when they first see her graceful pass at the golf ball. Ai's swing is slow, remarkably fluid and never finishes out of balance pure poetry in motion. That even-keel approach also characterizes her demeanor. Her emotional tempo is as consistent as her swing. Ai reminded us of one of our earlier students, Annika Sorenstam. Physically and emotionally she was always under control. That control both of the swing and of her emotions—had gotten lost.

Because of the enormous expectations, Ai had lost her tempo. She wasn't any less talented; it's just that the components of golf had come unstuck in the confusion and doubt around her. Ai had lost contact with her own uniqueness within the game. And part of what happens when you become unstuck is that you lose perspective; every problem becomes magnified in your mind and every obstacle thrown in your path appears to be twice as high as it really is. The tempo of your life is lost. You are out of rhythm.

Among the reasons why there is no such thing as a one-size-fits-all golf swing is that we all feel the rhythms of life differently. We all hear a different tune and we all feel a different beat. **Tempo is not something that can be explained to you, it is something you have to experience; it is**

something you have to feel. But tempo is also something you can learn to control. What happened with Ai was that she had let outside forces distract her from her own, true tempo. She had let the expectations of others disrupt the rhythm of her life—and her golf game.

"On the golf course I used to be so affected by how others were doing," Ai says, looking back at that down period. "In my personal life too I get influenced often by other people. VISION54 has taught me what my strengths and assets are and to be confident about them. I've learned from VISION54 that I need to imagine myself winning a tournament and playing well but doing so in as much detail as possible—what I see, what I feel, what I hear when I am playing great golf. And the more I practice this, the more I can connect myself with the golfer I aspire to be in a real-life, pressure-packed situation." In short, she was rediscovering her tempo—the rhythm that works for her.

Breakthroughs are always twofold: First there is the realization and then there is the actualization. Ai came to grasp that she had lost her way in the game by surrendering the rhythm and tempo of her life and game to the expectations of others. Once she realized this, she was ready to commit to several VISION54 disciplines that would help her address the manifestations of her "slump," for lack of a better word to mean merely temporarily losing your way in the game.

"When I lost my tempo [in 2007], I could only think of hitting as many balls as I could and working on my mechanics," Ai says. "But VISION54 gave me a variety of practice options to get it back. For example, swinging with varied tempo. I would start by hitting a shot at twenty-five percent of my normal tempo, and then fifty percent, and then seventy-five percent and finally my full tempo. I would swing with my eyes closed and do the Tai Chi swing, in which I would take about two minutes to complete one slow motion swing. In this way, I found my tempo, the tempo that works for me."

How different is this approach from the scrape-and-hit practice of mindlessly whacking balls, which many employ on the range? As Ai explored these VISION54 exercises, she not only rediscovered her swing, she gained a greater understanding of the forces that affect her on the golf course and disrupt her tempo. And as that understanding deepened, she was able to implement VISION54 techniques to help her maintain her tempo within a round of golf and under competitive pressure.

"I feel that tempo and tension are things that are always connected," Ai says. "During a round, tension can make your tempo quick. When that happens, I try to first focus on my tension to get my tempo back to where it should be." Off the course, Ai works on improving her tempo by closing her eyes and trying to focus her attention inward, and even hitting some shots on the range with her eyes closed. She hits shots at varying tempos with different clubs as she tries to *feel* her tempo so she can dial it in on the golf course.

There are many ways to get this feel. Kevin Streelman, a

PGA Tour player we are working with, will hit shots with different tempos in practice and then check the facts on his TrackMan, a golf radar that measures spin rate, club speed, launch angle and much more. Kevin found that dropping his tempo down a notch made the launch conditions of his shots better. He's the kind of person who likes to get scientific confirmation of the inner art of sensing tempo. For the elite player, tempo awareness is a great skill for controlling trajectories and spin rate. With slower tempo, the spin rate and the trajectory of the ball will be lower. Increase the tempo and they get higher.

While everyone has his or her own unique tempo that works best for that player, it is really more like a unique range of rhythms in which each player best functions. **Tempo is something you borrow rather than own. It is constantly in motion and changes depending on how your body and swing feel on any particular day.** When it's cold and windy, many swing too fast. In really hot and humid weather, some become sluggish. Self-talk can also affect tempo, as can your emotional resilience. Under tournament conditions, you might get an adrenaline rush or be bothered by the attention of the gallery. All these can affect tempo.

But no matter what is making your tempo fluctuate, the player who learns to feel that fluctuation has the ability to adjust it during the round and get back on track. You can get into the rhythm of this particular day. The key is to discover your tempo, become friends with it, learn how to feel it, always nurture that ability and realize that your ideal tempo changes from day to day within a comfort zone that works best for you, and even during a round.

Your tempo is your tempo. It defines you. More accurately, you define it. Your personality may demand a quick tempo or a slow tempo or any speed in between. Tom Watson's tempo is very different from that of Ernie Els; Yani Tseng's tempo is very different from Ai's. They have all recognized what works for them. What tempo produces your best sequence of motion? Learning the feel of your perfect tempo is a discovery process.

Studies show that great ball strikers have the same sequence of motion at impact, meaning that the hips, upper body, arms and club reach the impact area one after the other and in that order. Many golfers find their most efficient sequence of motion, without having to change their body or swing, by exploring different tempos. We have found that many golfers who are restricted in their hips or shoulders start to strike the ball better if they downshift to 75 percent or 80 percent of full tempo. That is something you will find out through experimentation. Perhaps you can make a more functional golf swing and hit the ball farther with slower tempo.

But the first task for you is to be able to recognize the feel of different tempos. Can you sense the difference between your full-tempo swing, three-quarter-tempo swing, half-tempo swing and one-quarter-tempo swing? Players lose their tempo and realize it after the round. They will say, "Man,

I just got really quick out there." But why don't you know that and stop that when it is happening? Well, you can if you are able to feel your tempo. That's a skill you can learn.

The important thing about practicing tempo is that as you become more familiar with what tempo works for you, you will become better when you are getting out of whack at feeling it and stop it. **Understanding tempo—feeling it— allows you to be better friends with your golf swing.** You can't take a metronome out on the course with you, but you can internalize tempo so you feel the rhythm that works best for you.

Many players benefit greatly from doing a few tempo exercises in warm-ups. It helps wake up the life of the swing and it monitors what tempo feels good for that particular day. We said in the Play Box chapter ("Leave Your Mind Behind") that Play Box mastery comes before all the other Essentials. Before you can access any mastery of tempo, you need first to have the skill of being present. If you are not present, you can't sense the first-person experience of tempo.

As Ai grew to better understand the physical impact that tension has upon her game, she also became more aware of some of the mental gymnastics to which she was victim. Chief among those was the role self-talk played in disrupting her tempo. "Self-talk" is that voice in your head that can exhort you on to great accomplishments, but can also plant the seeds of doubt that undermine success. It's a concept we explore more fully in Chapter 9, where we provide tools for managing it. But it is very instructive to take a look now at how that little voice disrupted Ai's tempo.

"When things are going well, [that voice] can make good things happen naturally," Ai says. "But when things are not going well, it can make everything go in the wrong direction, so it is scary. My self-talk is something that only goes on inside of me, so if I don't treat it correctly, it can get uncontrollable."

What Ai has come to understand is that the inner voice is not something to be afraid of. You own that voice. It is part of who you are. You can reason with it, argue with it, silence it and change its mind. "It's very simple, but VISION54 has taught me the importance of self-talk," says Ai. "It used to be something that 'happened' depending on the mood I'm in. But now I can recognize my self-talk and change it if I need to. I can stop it from changing my tempo."

The techniques Ai has learned to control self-talk are both unique and universal. They are unique because she has adopted practices that address her specific experiences with self-talk. They are universal because we all have that voice inside us telling us to be afraid or preparing us for failure by reminding us of past mistakes. It is up to us to tell the voice that the past does not have to be the future.

"I've gotten to analyze my self-talk depending on the type of emotion I'm feeling," Ai says. "Because of that, I can be in a certain situation on the course, be able to analyze my self-talk, and stay calm. I try not to make my self-talk too exaggerated. I don't tell myself, 'OK, you're going to birdie the next hole,' because that kind of talk can put pressure on me. Instead, if I'm in a situation where I am irritated, I tell myself, 'OK, Ai, talk to your caddie.' Or when my habit of going into the future happens, I try to laugh it off by saying, 'Are you going into the future again?' and make it humorous."

Working with Ai's father, Masuru, we helped Ai back from that difficult stretch after the 2007 Women's British Open at St. Andrews and through a 2008 season that had more disappointments than it had successes. As we entered the 2009 season, all of the components of Ai's game began to mesh. And again, by "components" we are talking about not just the physical activity of playing golf but also that big-picture approach entailing the whole person. Ai had found herself and was no longer a fractured golfer. She had put the pieces back together.

In July, Ai finished sixth in the 2009 U.S. Women's Open and then got her first LPGA victory in the next tournament, the Evian Masters in France. Over the next thirteen months, she won five more times on the LPGA Tour. Clearly, a crucial corner had been turned. She had silenced not only the doubts of those around her, but also the negative thoughts that sometimes shouted within her. What Ai found in VISION54 was not an external philosophy she applied but rather an internal understanding of who she is, which she employed on the golf course to maintain her tempo and maximize her potential.

When Ai played in Japan, she knew who she was. She was in touch with her tempo and rhythm. She was in sync. She lost that identity when she came to play in the United States, but got it back through VISION54. "Lynn and Pia have always stressed about 'Ai54' and its journey and how to create it," she says. "They have never compared me to anyone else. When I was in Japan, I created an Ai Miyazato that I wanted to be, but through VISION54, I feel more confident about myself and am more willing to present to everyone my true self."

And it is only by recognizing and realizing your own true self that you are able to achieve success. For Ai, regaining her tempo—both physically and emotionally—was a matter of reclaiming the control she had surrendered to the expectations of others. By recognizing the role of self-talk, she was able to gain greater control over it, and that helped her regain the tempo of her swing.

TEMPO EXERCISES

Here are the steps to reliable tempo. If you practice them, you can control your tempo when you need to on the golf course. Learn to recognize how 25 percent tempo, 50 percent, 75 percent and 100 percent feel for the full swing. Do the same for chipping, pitching and putting. Keep the tempo constant for the entire swing or stroke. Were you able to keep the tempo constant? Can you sense the difference? What tempo feels best for you with different clubs for different shots and for different days? Practice and nurture the awareness of tempo and the ability to adjust the tempo. Develop the ability to efficiently adjust your tempo.

- Hit five drives with 50 percent tempo, five 7-irons at 75 percent and five half swings with your wedge.

- Hit a full 9-iron. Identify the spot where it landed. Now hit every club longer than your 9-iron and make them land on the same spot. Use full swings and vary your tempo.

- Hit a three-quarter 6-iron with 75 percent tempo; hit a half swing with your 6-iron at 100 percent tempo. Do the same with a longer club and a shorter club.

- Practice different pitching distances and vary the tempo. How do you hit a twenty-five-yard pitch shot with four different tempos? Do this with four different distances.

- Putt three-footers with four different tempos. Do this four times.

- Hit a drive as hard as you can while finishing in balance; hit the softest lob shot possible; hit the hardest 5-iron you can while finishing in balance; hit the softest three-quarter 9-iron possible. How must you manage yourself between the shots to create the different tempos?

- Make full swings with any club and vary the tempos of your backswing and forward swing: Take it back at 25 percent tempo and swing forward at 75 percent; now try 100 percent back and 25 percent forward. Try many different combinations. Now hit three shots, keeping the preferred tempo throughout your entire swing.

- Putt three three-footers, alternating between dropping the ball in the front of the cup, charging to the back of the cup and falling in the middle of the cup. Do this four times.

- Hit five drives with the fastest tempo you can while still being able to finish in balance.

Functional Tempo: You can feel the difference between four different tempos, with five different clubs, and make good contact with the ball.

Masterful Tempo: For eighteen holes, you can be keenly aware of your tempo and adjust it efficiently when needed.

CHAPTER 6

Tame Your Tension

"If you asked me the single most important key to longevity, I would have to say it is avoiding worry, stress and tension. And if you didn't ask me, I'd still have to say it."

Comedian George Burns, who lived to be one hundred

SWING KEY: The greatest saboteur of the golf swing is tension. You can learn to control it.

There is nothing that can put your balance and tempo out of whack quicker than tension. This is the demon that comes between you and your golf swing. And it is a demon with which we all struggle. That is simply a fact of life—and golf is a part of life. Two keys are first to understand where in your swing tension is likely to reside, and second to develop the skills to manage that tension so you can play your best golf. You can't eliminate tension, but you can learn to manage it.

While tension can have its roots in your mind—a fear about the situation you are in, warranted or not, or simply indecision—it manifests itself in your body. Mental concern translates into physical tension. Literally, your body tenses up in certain areas, and that makes it extremely difficult to make a fluid golf swing once, let alone repeat that swing time after time. Tension in the swing or putting stroke ruins your technique. It's as simple as that.

First, let's talk about awareness. **We know tension exists in all of us, but where does it reside for you?** Some players have too much tension during the entire swing. Others have tension show up at specific points during the swing—the takeaway, the downswing, the weight shift or at impact, for example. For some, it shows up only under competitive pressure, while others find even the act of recreational golf stressful. **Mastery of technique is of no value if you do not learn tension awareness.**

Understanding the importance of tension awareness is crucial to playing peak-performance golf. This understanding is one of the keys to allowing you to create a holistic approach to the game, blending all of the Essential Playing Skills into one unified performer of the game of golf. To grasp the importance of this skill, all you have to do is watch the best players try to tame their nerves. Even the most skilled players are at times victimized by tension.

When a shot goes wrong, it is easy to focus in on the purely mechanical aspects of the game: "He came over the top on that swing" or "She took the club back too far on the inside." That's what we hear the television commentators say. But those are not mistakes the player makes all the time. Why now? Why in this situation? Why did the player come over the top or take the club back too far on the inside at this very moment when it mattered most?

Tension is the great instigator of disrupted technique and will first manifest itself in the Think Box, where stress will keep you from making a clear decision or keep you from making a full commitment to that decision. Then that tension crosses the Decision Line with you into the Play Box. In an absolute worst-case scenario, this is what has happened:

- You have made a poor decision in the Think Box about the shot you are going to play.

- There is a part of you that has doubts about the decision you have made, so you are not committed to your decision.

- Your mind is a jumble in the Play Box and you have completely lost contact with your Play Box Awareness.

- You make a swing that is out of balance and lacking your tempo, and the ball flies horribly awry.

Yes, we can go to the videotape and point out the flaws in the swing you have just made, but what the video doesn't show is the tension in your body and the way it has disrupted your mind. **If you focus only on the swing you have made when analyzing a result that did not go**

as planned, you are looking only at a small part of the puzzle. You have lost the big picture, the real picture, the complete view. What people like to call "choking" involves clutter, confusion and a lack of commitment more than merely a poor swing. In fact, they are the formula for a poor swing. Athletes in all sports talk about the importance of "slowing the game down." This means learning not to let tension disrupt the performance routine you have developed.

Tension is not merely a mental or physical component of the game, but rather the beast with a foot in both camps and therefore the single biggest obstacle to a fully integrated swing. It is easy to say tension begins with fear or nervousness or doubt about the situation at hand, but that out-of-control thinking process is also the result of specific physical activities taking place in your body when you are under stress—and they are physical activities you can control.

Barbara Bonney, the world-famous soprano who attended our school, began singing professionally in 1979 and, because her father was a teaching pro, played golf from the age of eight until she was twelve, at which time she shifted her focus to music. It wasn't until well into her adult life that she started to play the game seriously, as a diversion from professional and personal pressures.

"I took a year off from work when I got divorced, and playing golf kept me sane and fit," Barbara says. "During that year off, I was seriously thinking of becoming a teaching pro rather than returning to the music business, so I was working on my game very seriously. I liked the look of the VISION54 program, and actually speak Swedish, so I thought it would be fun to work with Pia and Lynn."

What she found was that VISION54 contains some startling similarities to the peak-performance approach she had to music. "I would say the whole VISION54 program was a reflection of the tools I use to teach my students singing: self-awareness, self-esteem, focus and relaxation, physical strength," says Barbara. "It was so interesting to compare the concepts because, at the end of the day, they are the same. Performance remains the same, whether it is on the golf course or on the stage of an opera house or concert hall. I think it is important to do the work in the studio or the range, then to walk out on stage or the first tee with your brain switched off. The only option is to follow your instincts and react to an ever-changing and evolving situation."

Stan Freimuth is a retired money manager who found out about VISION54 from a magazine article. He had a 15 handicap for six years before he attended our school. Through better management of his Tension Awareness and after two years learning our skills for managing his tension, Stan was able to bring his handicap down to 5. He and three friends return to our school for one day twice a year for a tune-up.

"I learned how to be my own coach and came to understand that what exists between my ears and in my gut is more important than the angle of my wrists," Stan says. "Now it astounds me how people always go immediately to the technical when they are struggling with their game. I feel now like I always have an awareness of the complete game, of the mental, emotional, physical and social as well as the technical."

Stan is someone who knows the importance of maintaining control and making clear, informed decisions. As a money manager, that was essential. In his job, he also knew the importance of navigating his way through stressful situations. But on the golf course he was not so good at those skills. Part of what Stan had to learn was to bring the discipline he applied in his job to the sport he loves. At work he was fearless, and he needed to learn how to become that person on the golf course.

"I had no idea how important this was before going to Pia and Lynn, which is a little embarrassing when you consider my job and what it required," Stan said. "Now when the wheels come off on the golf course, I don't think about my mechanics. I know that it always comes back to tension and I do breathing exercises. **The problem isn't a breakdown in my mechanics, but in what led to the breakdown in my mechanics.**"

Common places for tension to show up are in the hands, arms, shoulders and especially jaw. Now, who would think that the jaw would be a part of the body that could undermine your ability to make a fluid golf swing? But this is where science is our friend, and an extremely useful tool. Research shows that there are more nerve endings in the jaw than in any other part of the body.

If you grit your teeth and try to make a swing with a clenched jaw, you have likely started a chain reaction that will lead to a poor golf shot. Find some photos of Ben Hogan making a swing, especially some of the frozen images of him in the downswing. Look at his face. It is startling how relaxed he looks. There is no tension in his jaw. In fact, his entire body appears to be at peace. Part of that calm state is the complete trust he had in his swing, but that trust also came from the fact that he tamed his tension and that his body was not working against him.

Similarly, when Tiger Woods hits one of his wild shots, those who watch him play a lot can often tell, before the club head ever strikes the ball, that the result is not going to be good. When Tiger reaches for another gear, you can see it in his face; you can see his body tense as he "muscles up" to hit the ball harder. Lost is the breathtaking fluidity that is his swing at its best.

In the previous chapters we have talked about Play Box, Decision and Commitment, Balance, and Tempo. Tension can sabotage all of those Essentials. That's why Tension Awareness is one of the Essentials. The first step toward taming tension is understanding how it manifests itself in you. You can become aware of the tension level in your body by creating it during practice. The more you are aware of it, the more likely you are to tame it. And tension can be tamed.

Some players experience tension because they try to make swings that their body can't really do. In fact, isn't that a common source of tension in all aspects of our lives—when we try to be someone we aren't and do not honor the essence of our selves? Always celebrate who you are. The stress-free swing is made when you are working with yourself and not against yourself.

This is an important point to remember: **Anyone's swing improves when that person learns how to manage tension.** The less tense you are, the more fluid your swing will be—it's as simple as that. With better awareness and a little bit of practice, anyone can improve in this area. When are you tense? On the first tee with people watching? When you have an important putt or need to drive the ball in the fairway? And when you have identified those moments when tension is most likely to occur, how do you manage it?

For some of you, it's as simple as taking a few deep-belly breaths to get the tension out. Fuzzy Zoeller used to whistle while he walked the fairways. Lee Trevino would talk to whoever would listen. There is a lot of waiting-around time in golf and it brings to mind the old axiom: "Idle hands are the devil's playground." Tension can build during those idle moments. That's why you have to fill those moments with activities that release tension. Some of our players stretch or even jump in place. Others send their minds on vacations to happy places with comforting thoughts. Kevin Streelman focuses on grip pressure when he is looking to relax; Suzann Pettersen is aware that tension for her resides in her upper body and jaw, and focuses on relaxing those areas.

In our golf schools, we establish Tension Awareness through several different exercises. One is the Tai Chi swing. Tai Chi is a Chinese exercise art that involves extremely slow, graceful movements. We have our players make a complete golf swing at a speed at which it takes two to three minutes to complete the full swing. You can also do this Tai Chi swing with your eyes closed. As you concentrate on your movements, you will discover the parts of your swing where tension exists. You will feel where the tension lives.

When you have identified a tension spot—say it is at the top of the backswing—stop and slowly go back and repeat that portion of the swing. What do you need to do to lessen the tension in that part of your swing? How does the tension manifest itself? Do your shoulders tighten up or does your grip pressure change? Does an awareness of the location of the tension ease the tension or make it more intense? Monitor your body.

Here is an exercise you can do: Hit four shots with the same club, starting with an extremely light grip pressure and ending with an extremely tight grip pressure. Maintain the grip pressure you start with throughout the swing. Where in the spectrum of tightness does the grip work best for you? Do this exercise with all of your shots, including chips and putts. When you play, is your grip pressure constant or is it all over the map? Many players squeeze the club more tightly at takeaway or in the transition to the downswing or right before contact.

Now hit three shots with three different levels of tension in your upper body—the shoulders, arms and jaw. Try to be rubbery loose and try to be grit-your-teeth tense. Where in that spectrum of tension do you swing best? If your tension level changes on the golf course, do you become tighter or looser? Many golfers clench their jaw while swinging. Some players get twitchy with their wrists when making the putting stroke. Some people respond to pressure by getting lazy with their swing.

Learning the tension level you want to have in the Play Box is extremely important, and a key to achieving your desired level of tension is learning to manage tension between shots. Barbara Bonney taught us a great tip for managing tension in the jaw. Put your tongue behind your bottom front teeth. When you do that, the jaw drops and relaxes into a functional position. This literally prevents you from gritting your teeth. We will also have a player hit shots with a potato chip between his or her teeth, the goal being to execute the shot without biting through the chip. You can also concentrate on feeling a low center of gravity as you walk between shots, or you can exaggerate purging exhales in your breathing, rolling your shoulders or doing any other stretch that helps your body be more functional. These disciplines work; they reduce tension. Try them.

To pretend tension doesn't exist or that you are immune to it is pure folly. And to think that the same tension level is the optimal state for all golfers is to deny a core principle of VISION54: You are an individual first and a golfer second. What works for you doesn't necessarily work for everyone else, and what works for everyone else doesn't necessarily work for you. What is true for everyone is that tension sabotages the swing. Your specific tools for managing your tension will be determined by you through experimentation. You can never be a blank slate devoid of emotions when you hit a golf ball. Some people play best when they are in fifth gear—like Greg Norman—and some play their best when they are in second gear—like Nick Faldo. You have to find the gear in which you function best, and you have to learn the ability to shift from gear to gear.

TENSION AWARENESS EXERCISES

- Practice the Tai Chi golf swing. Make the entire swing in extremely slow motion, taking two to three minutes to complete one full swing. Pay attention to tension. Where in the swing do you feel tension?

  - Your grip?

  - Your back?

  - Your shoulders?

  - Your legs during the weight shift?

  - If you discover unwanted tension in any area of the swing, what can you do to reduce it?

- Hit full shots with four different grip pressures, from extremely light to extremely firm. Which grip pressure works best for your swing? Do the same for putting shots.

- Focus on the jaw, neck and shoulders. Hit three shots with three different tension levels. Hit with a slack jaw, a tense jaw and a normal jaw. When you are trying to relax your jaw, keep your tongue behind your lower front teeth. This will help. Which is best for you? Do the same for putting shots.

- Hit chip shots with an alternating range of grip pressure, going from one (as light as you can grip the club) to four (the tightest). Keep your grip pressure constant during the swing. Which is best for you?

- Hit chip shots alternating between tight tension in your arms and shoulders, average tension and very loose. Do this three times. What tension level makes you hit more solid chip shots?

- Hit shots with different tension levels in your lower body. Hit shots with a tension level of one to four in your thighs. Hit shots with a tension level of one to four in your toes. What do you notice?

- Hit four shots with your tongue behind your lower front teeth. Hit four shots with arms that feel like cooked spaghetti. Hit four shots while you feel your breathing.

- Next time you play, consciously do physical movements like stretching or yawning or deep breathing to release body tension between shots.

Functional Tension Awareness: You know where you have a tendency to create tension in your body. You can sense where it starts and lives.

Masterful Tension Awareness: You know what tension level works for you. You know where you have a tendency to create tension. You know how to change it before a round and during a round.

CHAPTER 7

Build Your Emotional Resilience

"I'll teach you to ride on the wind's back, and away we go!"

Peter Pan, who never grew up

SWING KEY: Greatness is not how you perform in good times; it is how you react in bad.

When the alarm sounds at six-thirty, Vikki Templeton blinks the sleep from her eyes and swings into action. First, she gets her two boys ready for school, and then she joins her husband, Greg, in the barn to help him finish milking their 180 cows. Depending on the time of the year and the weather, there is silage to process, weeds to spray and tractor work to be done before heading off at three-twenty to retrieve the boys from school. In a good week, Vikki can sneak in one round of golf.

Such is life on a dairy farm near Nar Nar Goon, a tiny town of five hundred people to the east of the Templetons'

home. About forty miles to the west is Melbourne, the sec-
ond-largest city in Australia. When Vikki gazes from her back
door, she sees their L-shaped farm spreading out below, a
tranquil, green-brown vista that demands intense attention
but provides enormous satisfaction. There are many days
when Vikki performs her farm work with thoughts of golf
occupying her head, and those thoughts always bring a smile.

Vikki is accompanied on her chores by Lady, her constant
companion, while the other farm dog, Buddy, prefers to lie
around thinking about work. Another pet, a budgerigar bird,
flies free from her cage all day, picks food off plates, tries to
bathe in the sink while Vikki cooks dinner and gets really
loud if she feels she's being ignored. It is a demanding life in
an idyllic setting. The rhythm of farm life is built around the
satisfaction of a job well done.

Australians live a lot of their lives outdoors. The country is
populated by a sports-passionate people, and for a country of
only 20 million, one-sixteenth the size of the United States, it
has produced an astonishing number of great golfers, including Hall of Fame members Peter Thomson, David Graham,
Greg Norman and Karrie Webb. Vikki, while not possessing
those accomplishments, is world-class in her passion for life
and for the game of golf.

Vikki started playing the game when she was sixteen years
old but played very irregularly, without a lesson or a handicap.
Then, when she was in her late thirties, she decided that one
round a week, when possible, would be a great break from

farming. The more she played, the more she loved the game. She learned about VISION54 by reading golf magazines, and bought our first two books in September 2007. Then one of those happenstances occurred that make you believe life dances to an unheard tune and a faintly felt rhythm.

Greg proposed that they go to a seminar on cows in Germany. Vikki said they didn't both need to attend and offered this alternative: "If you go, can I pick something else for me?" she asked. And that's how Vikki ended up attending our program in Phoenix. At our school, Vikki learned the factors that allowed her to access the joys of surrendering to her love of the game of golf. It was there that she learned to embrace the journey and there that she learned about the tools for emotional resilience that have not only allowed her to enjoy golf more, but also made her a better player.

Emotional resilience is all about learning how to keep your head in the game, and it is an essential component to great golf. This is not as one-sided as it sounds, since to manage your emotions is to understand the impact that emotions have on both the physical and mental aspects of you, and to recognize how that influences your performance. Emotional resilience is also about not letting unpleasant experiences in the past affect present performance. That resilience involves learning how to build a reserve of positive emotions by focusing on the good you have experienced, and learning how to use the good you have experienced to make yourself better.

Emotions release hormones that affect the access you have to your higher brain functions. Simply put: Anger makes you stupid, while joy allows you to access a peak-performance state. You can learn to create a reserve of energy that lets you stay focused and coordinated for the entire round of golf. Bad bounces and bad weather are beyond your control, but you can learn to manage your emotional state when these things happen.

Soon after Vikki went through our program, we got an e-mail from her saying she had won her first scratch tournament ever. She plays off an 18 handicap and has a career-best 82 gross on a par-72 course. That's pretty remarkable, really, when you consider she had played regularly for only about four years.

What changed the most for Vikki, what deepened, was her understanding of the beauty of the game and her realization that a large part of the allure of golf is the magical way in which it mirrors life. She deepened her relationship with golf, and this gave her greater control over her emotional state both on and off the golf course. Simply put, a happy person plays better golf. The greater attachment Vikki felt to the game, the higher her level of performance.

"My VISION54 is represented in the song 'Piece of Sky' by Barbra Streisand: 'The more I live, the more I realize the less I know,'" says Vikki. "You never stop learning, and you can learn from any situation, good and bad. I think if you stop learning, you stop living. I love it." By getting in touch with that joy, by releasing that passion, Vikki's performance on the golf course improved. What she learned from us was that there are specific, intentional ways you can create that euphoric state—and ways to avoid the destructive downward spirals.

It is essential to manage your emotions to play your best golf. This is one of those nonnegotiable rules of peak-performance golf. Just imagine one of those endless lines of dominoes when someone is trying to break the world record for longest lines. When the first domino is pushed, they all start falling, taking each other down one by one. That's the way your emotions interact with your physical and mental functioning. But you have the power to control whether the chain reaction is positive or negative.

Positive emotions release DHEA, which is a hormone that functions like a lubricant to the brain, allowing you to slip into full access of higher brain function. It is a state in which you make clearer, more informed and more committed decisions. You also have full access to your visual centers, fine motor skills and the executive center of the brain. That's the happy place in which you can achieve great things. This is where great golf shots live. You know that feeling when you step up to a golf shot and you are certain you are going to hit it well? That's this state—and it doesn't have to be elusive.

DHEA doesn't guarantee greatness, but it does allow you to have full access to your ability and makes it possible to sustain being great. DHEA is a performance-enhancing drug and it's free and legal inside of you. All you have to do to trigger its release is to genuinely feel a positive emotional state.

Negative emotions release cortisol, which is a hormone that blocks full access to higher brain functions. Cortisol levels that are too high inhibit the functioning of the thalamus, a part of the brain. As a result, you only access the reptilian and mammalian parts of your brain. You think like a dog, and you play like a dog—except you probably don't have as much fun as a dog. You think poorly, behave poorly and perform poorly. This is a disruptive state that can last six to ten hours—long enough to sabotage your golf game and a good part of the rest of your day.

It doesn't really matter if your personality is introverted or extroverted; these hormones are still being released and affecting the access to your higher brain functions. We all experience joy and we all get angry, and we show that joy and anger in different, highly individual ways. What does matter is that you understand and honor who you are, and that you learn an ability to "go with the flow" and shift your state when necessary.

Do you play your best with higher or lower adrenaline levels? Are you more like Tiger Woods, Suzann Pettersen, Sergio Garcia and Christina Kim? They need a lot of adrenaline to perform at their best. Or are you more like Annika Sorenstam, Ernie Els, Catriona Matthew and Retief Goosen, who all play better with less adrenaline? If you are not clear where you belong, go back to a time when you played well and analyze it. How were you then—amped up or mellow? You can also experiment playing with higher and lower adrenaline levels and record what happens.

We know some players who say they perform better when they are angry, since they finally get enough adrenaline flowing. But we already said that anger makes us stupid. So how can you get to that state of high adrenaline without the negative side effect of cortisol? Well, remember Sergio Garcia as a rookie playing in front of Tiger Woods at the 1999 PGA Championship, galloping out onto the fairway with a big smile on his face after hitting that ball from behind a tree? That is happy adrenaline. We have tools that will allow you to manage your adrenaline levels without triggering the release of the bad chemicals.

Often, when things are going badly on the golf course, you become a spectator to your own demise. How silly is that? It's your life, your golf—take control. Adrenaline levels can be changed in a few seconds through breathing exercises and other physical tools. For example, take long, deep cleansing breaths—breathing in to the count of three and breathing out to the count of six. This will immediately lower your adrenaline level and calm your nervous system.

If your play has become lethargic and you need a boost, a more rapid breathing pattern will increase your adrenaline level. You can also raise your adrenaline level by doing jumping jacks or running sprints. We know players who will do this as part of their pre-round routine in order to get their adrenaline level up. Trust us, there will be people who think you have gone off your rocker. But also trust us on this: It works.

Ideally, you should come off the golf course with more energy and feeling better about yourself than when you started, no matter the result of your play. How often can you say that happens for you? **Part of your pre-round routine should be to take an emotional inventory of yourself and evaluate your emotional state.** Do you need to take it up a notch today or bring it down? This will vary from day to day, no matter who you are. With practice, you will learn to be aware of the fluctuations in your emotional state during a round and develop strategies to manage it.

We have said that if your cortisol is too high, it will affect you for many hours. Remember that it's the same for DHEA. Cortisol and DHEA come from the same base molecules. So if you have a lot of cortisol, you will have less DHEA and vice versa. If you start the day or the round with a lot of DHEA, that is long-lasting as well, and that is a good thing.

That is what we call emotional resilience. It doesn't mean you don't hit bad shots, but it does help you manage the situation and have access to the whole brain when you do have disappointing outcomes. **Resilience can be seen as the ability to sustain competence under stress and in challenging conditions.** This hardiness allows you to stay in the game. It's the ingredient of mental toughness that allows you to be unflappable and maintain the ability to stay calm and focused while others are experiencing chaos.

A great way to keep track of your emotional state is to draw a cross on the scorecard or in the yardage book. The vertical axis is your adrenaline, with high adrenaline at the top and low at the bottom. The horizontal axis represents your emotions. The left side is DHEA (the good stuff) and the right side is cortisol (the bad stuff). Put an X where you play your best golf. Are you happy and contented when the X is just under the midline on the adrenaline axis? Or are you joyous playing when you are higher on the adrenaline axis? Only you know.

After each hole, write down where you are on this grid. Put a 1 on the grid after the first hole, a 2 after number two, etc. This will give you an awareness of where you go emotionally during a round. Let's say you play your best golf when your emotions are in the upper left quadrant. After five holes, you notice that you are down to the right, almost feeling like you don't care what's happening. What are you going to do? Do you need to get more adrenaline in you? The point is that all of us will, at times, slip into the cortisol side of the grid. How quickly can you become aware of this slide and do something to shift your emotional state before your cortisol levels get too high and you are cooked for the round?

When you listen to Vikki talk about the revelations she has had about golf through our school, you can't help but wonder if her experiences as a farmer have aided her insights. By watching the seasons change and being attuned to the cycle of life, Vikki was well aware that there are forces of nature beyond our control to which we must surrender. You can plant the seeds, but you can't make it rain.

Our energy must be focused on those aspects of life we can influence through careful preparation, concentrated understanding and total commitment. That's a key concept to emotional resilience: Work on what you can control and don't worry about what you can't control. This is a bit of emotional triage central to VISION54. Don't borrow trouble by worrying about that which you can't control. There are enough controllable things that need our attention.

"What I learned from *Every Shot Must Have a Purpose* is that golf is a game that is a continually changing journey," says Vikki. "Golf changes shot to shot, day to day, course to course, and to enjoy the ride to its full potential, you must understand all its elements and totally commit to its actions. Golf evolves around your ability not only to understand the technical side of the game, but also to grasp the other five elements of the game that affect you," says Vikki. "To understand the way you interact with all the elements—physical, technical, emotional, mental, social and spiritual—affects the way you hit that little white ball."

Certainly, a high-functioning individual is someone who has integrated all aspects of human existence—the physical, technical, mental, emotional, social and spiritual. Your state of being affects your physiology, and therefore it affects your performance. This is true in all areas of human activity, not just golf. **By controlling your emotional state, by managing your emotional resilience, you increase the possibility of the total integration that leads to peak-performance play.** You have greatly increased your chances of success.

Your emotions affect how you think, how you see, how you reason and how you perceive the world around you. They also affect your motor skills. We helped Vikki with the tempo of her golf swing, but it was what she learned about her relationship with the game that really enabled her to improve. Great players—without exception—are in love with the game. They are also not afraid of failing or looking silly. When they are not playing well, they are able to tap into their passion for the game and salvage a decent round by managing their emotions. They rarely give up on a round of golf.

"The actions we must commit to also interact with our performance," says Vikki. "These actions—strategy-making, decision-making, commitment to the decision, focus, execution and reaction to the shot—are all interconnected with the elements. It is your ability to pull these elements and actions together that will determine your potential to get the ball in the hole in the fewest shots. And when we practice, we must look at all the elements, not just the technical, so that when we hit the course, we can fully commit to the 'trust element,' so that we can reach our own VISION54 goals."

That last statement is crucial. While our approach evolved

as a challenge to players to make not just par on every hole, but rather birdie—and thus shoot a 54 on a par-72 course—it is really a metaphor for individual peak-performance goals. Everyone has his or her own VISION54 objectives. What are yours? Is it to break 100, 90, 80, 70, 60? What is essential is not where you are going but how you are going to get there. That's what we provide—not a single direction, but several roads. Staying engaged with and committed to the process will create greater emotional resilience for you.

"The main thing I learned from VISION54 it that it is not only about golf, but also about life," says Vikki. "Life is often mirrored in your golf. The lessons learned in VISION54 are so transferable to your everyday life. One thing I have learned is to only concentrate on what I can control and not dwell on the uncontrollable. When I look out my back door, I see our farm spreading out below and the work that I need to do for the day. Scary some days—until you focus on the controllable and forget the uncontrollable."

Vikki is clearly a woman of considerable passion, and because of that, she was extremely receptive when she attended our school. Her heart was open to the game of golf. That's a huge advantage to have. **An important step toward developing emotional resilience and gaining control of your emotions on the golf course is allowing yourself to feel the game at your very core—in the heart of your being.**

That was easier for Vikki than for many because of who she

is. But it is a state that anyone can reach. For some, managing their emotional resilience might be the most challenging—and most important—of the Essentials. For everyone, it is the doorway to achieving peak performance in the Play Box.

We are not saying that you will never get angry, sad or frustrated. Of course you will, you are a human being. But we are saying that you can learn to recognize what is happening earlier in the process and stop the emotional chain reaction before the hormones that shut down access to your higher brain function take over. Emotional resilience is the positive capacity of people to cope with stress, like putting that drive that went out of bounds behind you.

Emotional resilience also has a cumulative effect on your performance. Positive emotions cause DHEA and other neu ropeptides to be released into the body. This neurobiological base makes you more adaptive to disruptions and more resistant to getting off track with your game. You're able to stay focused and remain aware of options, and maintain access to good feelings even when you feel stressed. You literally have more chemical resistance when others are succumbing to the pressure. It's not just a good idea; it's a neurobiological state that you can create that directly affects your ability to perform. This emotional sturdiness allows you to keep your head in the game. It's the neurobiology of how the tough get going when the going gets tough.

Just understanding the physical process of all this has been beneficial to many players with whom we have worked. Lots

of avid golfers who have been at the game a long time without getting the results they want slip into a high-cortisol and
low-adrenaline state. They become apathetic, find it boring
to practice and even get a little depressed. Learning about
emotional resilience becomes critical to rekindling the spirit
of their game. This low-performance state can easily happen
to those players who equate their score to who they are as a
person. They can't separate who they are from what they do.
If they play well, they are happy. If they play poorly, they are
miserable. This way of interpreting the game is not sustainable. If you are not careful, you might think that you are your
score. Actively creating more DHEA is essential to staying in
a good state for golf and for life.

EMOTIONAL RESILIENCE EXERCISES

- Write down ten things you are grateful for, and
  genuinely feel that gratitude.

- Hit ten shots and fall in love with each shot before
  stepping into the Play Box.

- Hit some shots with lots of adrenaline and some shots
  with very little adrenaline. Which makes you swing
  better? You can change your adrenaline state through
  breathing exercises and physical movements in the Think
  Box. Do the same on the putting green.

- Hit fifteen different shots, and before each shot spend
  fifteen extra seconds genuinely feeling something

positive in your heart in the Think Box. A PGA Tour player we coach calls this "accessing active gratitude" before he enters the Play Box.

- Hit ten shots while you smile at the golf ball. Keep smiling the entire swing.

- Hit ten putts, smiling for the entire stroke.

- Practice hitting shots with high, medium and low adrenaline levels. Jog or do jumping jacks to get your adrenaline up. Sit down and breathe deeply with long exhales to get your adrenaline down. At what adrenaline level do you perform the best?

- Write down ten things that create DHEA for you. What makes you feel positive emotions? At least five of these things need to be things you can do while playing on the golf course.

- Play on the course and monitor your adrenaline and emotional state after each hole. Do it with the grid the way we explained in this chapter.

- Play on the course, and after each shot, for ten seconds, access something that makes you feel positive emotions.

Functional Emotional Resilience: You can catch yourself feeling negative emotions on the golf course and you are able to shift your emotions during the same hole, or before starting the next hole.

Masterful Emotional Resilience: For eighteen holes you are neutral or happy. You feel that you come off the golf course with more energy, with more DHEA and feeling better about yourself than when you started, no matter the outcome.

CHAPTER 8

Store Positive Memories, Manage the Others

"I use memories, but do not allow memories to use me."

Shivas Sutras

SWING KEY: Store your good shots so you can revisit them.

D o you remember that time when you were a child and touched the hot stove, your hand recoiling in pain? Mom ran over, gently kissed the tip of your finger and gave you some ice to ease your discomfort. Everything about that experience became part of who you are and what you know about the world around you. Without having to consciously file away the information, you learned that hot stoves hurt and that your mother will always be there for you.

Emotional memories like the one above get stored in the

amygdala part of the brain. That's the way we all are wired. Filed away was the fact that Mom loves you. Also filed away was the fact that you shouldn't touch the stove when it is turned on. Everything that happened was automatically recorded in your memory bank as an essential survival skill. Filing away your great golf shots is an Essential Playing Skill, as is managing the memory of your poor shots. The better you connect to your positive memories, the more likely you are to create great new positive memories. The saying "Confidence breeds confidence" is literally true—if you store positive memories.

While the stove incident is an impulse memory based on pain and out of your control, there are memories that are more voluntary, that you can control. This is where you establish the mechanics of confidence. Your brain is wired to remember the bad experiences more easily than the good as a survival skill. To reach your potential in golf, you have to learn to store your good shots by establishing an emotional connection with them. This is how to create a "go" signal when you are walking up to a shot.

Beth Brown is the director of curriculum and research at The First Tee, the youth development program supported, in part, by golf's governing bodies, as well as an LPGA teaching professional with a PhD in education. Like many of us, her passion for golf is tied to childhood memories. When she was twelve years old, Beth would walk eighteen holes in the morning with her red vinyl bag, work at her dad's Dairy

Queen for four hours in the middle of the day and then play another eighteen holes before dark.

But when she came to our school in 2008 she had lost that emotional connection to the game. She was no longer having fun on the golf course. "My first 'aha' moment occurred when Lynn and Pia asked me, 'Why do you play golf?'" Beth says. "I responded that I was still trying to remember what I loved about the game. I thought if I could rediscover that passion I had as a child, that joy, then surely I would fall in love with the game again."

When Beth thought about it, she realized that at least since college she had linked her enjoyment of the game to her results. If she didn't play well, she didn't have as much fun on the golf course. The golf memories Beth had stored when she was twelve were about process—the pure joy of the game. The stored memories since college had been about results— the pressure of the competitive game. She was not the same person as the twelve-year-old Beth and she had to learn to find her love of the game in a different way.

"From that moment forward, it was about being in the present and exploring what I love now," Beth says about her "aha" breakthrough. She set about trying to learn who the now-Beth is and what makes her most happy on the golf course. "I know I play my best golf when I slow down and let go," Beth says. "I learned I need to spend less time in the Think Box; create a peaceful connection to the target; and maintain my target connection all the way through the swing."

This is a very different person from the twelve-year-old Beth who was happy just to be out on the golf course walking thirty-six holes. That was pure and simple play. The adult Beth has a much more complicated relationship with the game. Beth came to understand that as a child she had successfully stored those glorious memories that were the basis for her connection to the game—her love of the game. But her current memory bank had become much different.

When you are twelve and the game is as simple as "hit the ball, go find it and hit it again," it is easy to store positive memories. For one thing, there are fewer negative memories to compete with the positive memories, since the game is pretty much all about play and not about work or competition. The adult Beth had to learn that her connection to the game is different now and that she needs to actively work on storing different positive memories.

Part of what we do at our school is get everyone out on the course, where the game is really played. We were walking with Beth during a round one day, and when she would hit a good shot, one of us would ask, "How was that experience?" If she said it was a good experience, we would then ask, "Did you store that shot inside of you?" This process occurred several times during the round.

"Then Pia decided to challenge me," says Beth. "I guess she wasn't buying my story. This time she said, 'Did you really?' I suddenly stopped walking off the tee and realized I had seen and felt the shot, but it was more like someone else had done it. I had observed it, but I hadn't experienced it."

Beth realized that this practice of living life as a third-person observer rather than experiencing life as a first-person participant was not unique to her golf. "I'm certain I do this in all areas of my life," Beth says. "When I do something well or when others compliment me, I see it, hear it and know that I did it, but I don't really take it in, absorb it, experience it inside myself and lock it away in my memory."

Beth needed to learn the Essential of storing positive memories—how to take ownership of her great shots and her good shots, how to make them live in her memory like the touch of a hot stove—only this time as positive experiences that can be relived over and over rather than as a bad experience to be avoided. **Storing positive memories is a skill that can be learned.** As with all of the Essentials, this is something under your control. That is why it is an Essential. Beth developed her own personal tools.

"The result on the golf course has been that after good shots I anchor them in my memory by twirling my club, admiring the shot and just slowing down and enjoying the moment," Beth says. "I recall these shots much more readily now because so many more are first-person experiences that I have stored away." Think of great players. They all have a way of stamping a great shot into their memory bank, whether it is a fist pump, a raised club or even a hop and a skip. Juli Inkster used to dance when she made a key putt.

Your emotions store events as memories, and these memories affect your future performance. So your challenge is to control your emotional reaction to your shots. You want to have a strong emotional reaction to a good shot and a neutral emotional reaction to a bad shot. One exercise we like to have players do is to say aloud something positive or factual about every shot they hit—no matter the result. Can you hit a big slice and then say: "I was totally committed to my playing focus" or "Gee, it's a beautiful day"? Try it! You'll find it more challenging than you think—and extremely useful. You can learn not to get angry over your bad shots.

When you are on the golf course, feel all the things you do well, so you can store those memories. **Live the great shots as first-person experiences, but analyze the shots that don't work from a third-person objective perspective.** That way you can learn from those experiences without storing them in your memory bank. For every shot, you can either store the experience or view it objectively. That is something that is under your control.

Some people are demonstrative with their post-shot reactions and it is very easy to see if they are pleased, angry or disappointed with the result. Others are more difficult to read and might look calm on the outside while they are really experiencing the same turmoil as the extroverted person. When it comes to storing memories or establishing emotional resilience, the impact is the same no matter if your reaction is extroverted or introverted.

We originally met Beth because of her involvement with the First Tee, for whom we were consulting. A large part of the great work being done by the First Tee is emphasizing to young people the values and life skills learned through golf—including honesty, decision-making and respect. Beth learned another life skill to use in her teaching—remembering the good shots and neutralizing the bad. And, like all of the Essential Playing Skills, this truly is a life skill.

"The result in my life, away from golf has been significant as well," Beth says about learning how to manage her memories. "I catch myself glossing over a positive experience—observing it from outside myself—and I just stop and say something to myself like, 'Hey! *You* did that! Stop and enjoy it! That was incredible.' Also, when I get compliments or positive reinforcement from others, I sometimes share those comments with my husband. Saying the comment out loud helps me store it away in my long-term memory."

Some players set such high standards for themselves that they store very few shots in their memory bank because, to them, very few shots are "perfect." Ben Hogan used to say he hit only one or two shots a round that went exactly the way he planned. **The key is to store those shots that are "good enough" and not let an obsession with perfection cloud your memory bank.** Once, in discussing the overuse of the word "great," the inimitable Fred Couples said: "Hey, I'm not great, I'm good; but good's not bad." Exactly. Recognize those "good enough" shots with an emotion, embrace that emotion and store that positive memory. This is not about becoming cocky; it is about becoming confident. In fact, it's how you create confidence.

When you are standing over a shot, you want to be remembering the times you pulled off such a shot, not the times you didn't. For that reason, it is just as important to learn how to stay neutral when you hit a shot that you don't like as it is to celebrate those you do like. To overreact to poor shots is to store a memory that can come back to haunt you at the most inopportune time. Embrace the good; be clinical about the bad.

There is no doubt this is a lot easier said than done. "I wish my pre-shot routine was the end of the story," Beth says. "But for me what happens after the shot is critical. My nature is to be very hard on myself and expect nothing less than perfection." Certainly, expecting perfection is a recipe for disaster. How you react when you have a result that is less than satisfying will have a major impact on how you will handle a similar shot in the future. If you overreact—get angry, throw a club or just berate yourself internally—you are more likely to remember—and repeat—that shot next time you are in a similar situation.

Don't deny that you have hit an unsatisfying shot; just learn how to control your emotional response to it. **We can't control what happens to us, but we can control how we react to what happens to us.** Every shot you hit has two possibilities of storage. You can either store, or stay neutral to the outcome of the shot or how you did with the process of the shot. When a poor shot occurs, instead of focusing on the outcome, focus on how you did with your Play Box state or how you did with your commitment to your decision.

The stored memory works in this way: When you come to a similar situation in the future, your amygdala searches for matches on a subconscious level (a hot stove, a three-foot putt with a left-to-right break). If it finds a match that was negative, it will give you a physiological warning in the form of apprehensive thoughts, tension, a pounding heart. This is great in terms of your survival, but not so much in terms of that three-foot putt.

There is so much talk in golf about pre-shot routines, and there is no question they are important (although sometimes overly exaggerated). But just as important—and this is key to remember—is your post-shot routine. How you react to a shot determines how your brain will store the memory of that shot. This is simple science. We know this to be true.

Dr. Barbara Fredrickson, a social psychologist and the Kenan Distinguished Professor of Psychology at the University of North Carolina at Chapel Hill and author of the book *Positivity*, discovered that experiencing positive and negative emotions in a three-to-one ratio leads people to a tipping point beyond which they naturally become more resilient to adversity and effortlessly achieve what they once could only imagine. Her extensive research concluded that positive emotional memories carry far more benefits than most of us suspected.

She categorizes two classes of these benefits into what she calls the broaden-and-build theory. First, when we experience a positive emotion, our vision literally expands, allowing us to make creative connections, see our oneness with others, and face our problems with clear eyes (the broaden effect). Second, as we make a habit of seeking out these pleasing states, we change and grow, becoming better versions of ourselves, developing the tools we need to make the most out of life (the build effect).

And strikingly, these twin benefits of positive emotions obey a tipping point: When positive emotions outnumber negative emotions by at least three to one, these benefits accrue, yet below this same ratio, they don't. Simply put, you can learn to bypass your amygdala's automatic default operations, in much the same way you choose to tap different buttons on a computer to go to a different screen. React in the default mode and your amygdala can heat up a situation by placing you in a far too sensitive mood, flooding your brain with cortisol and causing you to overreact. You have to learn ways to efficiently stay neutral to those memories.

Caught under attack, you'll respond accordingly, whether the attack is real or perceived, unless you intervene to help your brain. Because of your amygdala, you can develop and use different strategies to create calm under pressure, and as you build emotional patterns for dealing with stressors, you begin to see the usefulness of the patterns. Pragmatically, you learn to deal more calmly with the undesirable outcomes and bad bounces. You don't have to be a victim of your stored fear response. Embrace the three-to-one ratio as your baseline and you'll start to tame the hot amygdala and rewire your post-shot responses to something that is productive and performance enhancing.

We know players who have a short fuse, panic easily and generally make mountains out of molehills. People with the hottest amygdalas are the drama queens, rage-a-holics, worrywarts and chronic complainers among us. When the amygdala gets stuck in overdrive, it widens the negative neural pathways in our brain. Our minds become overrun with negative thoughts and we worry, picturing over and over what we don't want to happen, creating anxiety and unhappiness in our lives and our golf games. How do you think you perform in such a state?

The hot amygdala is also how the yips are created neurologically. Studies done by Dr. Richard Davidson, director of the Laboratory for Affective Neuroscience at the University of Wisconsin–Madison, demonstrate that thinking new and different thoughts creates new neural pathways. When we change our thinking to support our happiness, the negative neural pathways shrink and the positive neural pathways widen. This makes it easier and more automatic for us to think more positively.

You can learn to have far greater control over what you remember. Have you ever had a discussion with a high school friend about some long-past event that you remember as being either extremely positive or extremely negative? The memory is crystal clear in your mind. You can recall every detail of the incident—down to what you were wearing, how the room smelled and what music was playing. Then you find out that your friend barely remembers what you are talking about.

What's the explanation? Certainly, the event occurred. But the event had a bigger emotional impact on you at the time—embarrassment or joy—than it had on your friend. As a result, the memory lives in each of you far differently. For you, it is written in indelible ink; for your friend, it exists as a faded pencil mark. Perhaps one of you overreacted or one of you underreacted, but the emotional impact of the event at the time determined the degree to which you each stored it in your memory.

When we are neutral, factual or objective in our post-shot reaction, the brain won't store the memory of the shot in the amygdala as strongly. That's a good way to react to bad shots, and a bad way to react to good shots. Some players need to be better at storing positive shots; others need to learn to manage their reaction to their bad shots. Often the negative response is so automatic that it's difficult to break the habit. Some golfers benefit from training themselves to say something factual after an undesirable outcome: If the ball missed the cup on the left edge, instead of saying, "I can't putt," you could respond with something like, "I stroked the ball really solidly."

Others do better to start singing or humming right after they finish the swing or stroke. Suzann Pettersen, whom we coached for several years, would start counting immediately after a swing to break her anger habit. Sometimes at Tour events she would come up close to the ropes and say, "One thousand twenty-four, one thousand twenty-five, one thousand twenty-six"! Suzann, like many players, at first thought the emotional management skills were only for etiquette reasons. But when the players understand how it affects their performance, confidence, energy level, ability to swing well, decision-making and visualization—then it becomes a lot more interesting and important to them.

Write your great golf shots in your memory in permanent ink. Tattoo them onto your brain. Have them live in you as an endless celebration of the joy this game can bring. The bad shots are something that happens—just a part of life, like a parking ticket or a rainy day. In no way should those shots ever be regarded as more important than the good shots. Remember, you didn't stop baking cakes just because the stove burned you once. The memory of how delicious the cake tasted lives too strongly in you to ever let that happen. Make your great golf shots your emotional dessert. Savor the flavor—and remember them.

STORING MEMORIES EXERCISES

- Hit twenty different shots while being objective in your post-shot reactions.

- Hit twenty different shots while being very positive in your post-shot reactions, no matter the outcome. Find something about which you can be genuinely happy related to the outcome of the shot or the process of hitting the shot.

- After each shot during a practice session, if you did not like the outcome, say something aloud that is objective, neutral or simply factual about the shot.

- After each shot during a practice session that you hit great, good or good enough, spend fifteen extra seconds feeling genuine pleasure about it in your heart.

- Hit ten great, good or good-enough shots and feel a positive emotion in your post-shot routine.

- Play six holes and be 100 percent objective after you finish each shot. Talk like a scientist, count, skip, hum a song.

- Experiment with different anchors to store positive shots. An anchor can be an extroverted display or an introverted acknowledgment. Is it an inward smile? A fist pump? A warm feeling in the stomach? A verbal anchor? What works best for you to create a connection with your good shots in order to store their memory?

Functional Storage of Memory: You are able to catch yourself reacting in a negative way and turn it around to a factual and objective perspective.

Masterful Storage of Memory: For eighteen holes, you have either been objective/neutral or positive/happy in each post-shot reaction. Your criterion for being happy about a shot is when it's good enough (not perfect!).

CHAPTER 9

Drown Self-Talk with Useful Ideas

"It's not enough to rage against the lie; you've got to replace it with the truth."

Bono, rock musician and social activist

SWING KEY: You can control what that voice says to you.

We all move within a circle of life that includes thoughts, feelings and behavior, each affecting the other. Harmony is created by blending those elements, making a soup of delicious ingredients in a perfect balance. Part of the struggle to maintain that balance is keeping your focus on that which you can control and not letting your mind be distracted by those elements of life beyond your control—those ingredients that are going to be part of the soup stock of your life no matter what.

It is essential to remember that what you pay attention to—what you focus on—tends to grow in importance in your mind and in your world. In many ways, it is through this attention that you validate the existence of your feelings and make the past a part of your future. One of the ways that happens involves how you react to events in your life. And it involves how you react to your reactions.

We all have that voice within us that evaluates our actions and passes judgment on those actions. That voice also has a major influence on future actions by talking to you as you prepare for those actions. This self-talk can be a positive force, but more often for most of us, it is a negative factor. It is up to you to manage your self-talk. One of the most fundamental skills in life is to learn how to manage the conscious mind. That voice affects all we do. Scattered and distracted self-talk creates a scattered and distracted golf swing.

Denying the existence of self-talk is a futile activity, just as it is absurd to deny tension or fear. It's there, it exists and it is not going to go away. The key is managing that talk, not eliminating it. That sometimes not-so-little voice in your head that can create doubt and confusion exists—pure and simple. You have to acknowledge that it is nearly impossible to quiet it completely for long periods of time. This is a trained skill very few can do. But you need to train yourself to sense instead of think for the few seconds you are in the Play Box. **You can replace the destructive noise with a positive song.** The importance of being fully engaged with all your senses while in the Play Box cannot be overemphasized. You must be alive in the moment when in the Play Box and not living in your head.

Debra Oberg is a businesswoman from New Jersey with a single-digit handicap. She is also a cancer survivor who has overcome doubts and fears that were not only whispered into her ear but also shouted at her in the cruelest voice life allows. Through VISION54, Debra gained a new perspective, not just on golf, but on how to handle those seeds of doubt our mind loves to sow in our confidence and optimism.

"I had faced cancer and divorce after fifteen years of marriage just prior to meeting Lynn and Pia," said Debra, who was told about our school by two-time New Jersey State Women's Amateur champion Donna Young, a friend of hers. "VISION54 transformed my life, my golf and my heart," Debra said. "VISION54 gave me the tools to overcome my bad tendencies and not allow those bad thoughts to creep in." Note that Debra said, "not allow those bad thoughts to creep in," and did not say, "made those bad thoughts go away." That is a hugely important level of understanding on her part. One way to manage negative self-talk is to replace it with something.

There is science to what we are saying. Beliefs are nothing more than specific neural patterns in your brain, thoughts that are so ingrained they have become automatic. They exist not because they are "the truth" but because someone put them there often enough or in dramatic enough fashion that they have stuck. They have become your truth. We are all constantly bombarded by a huge number of stimuli. Since we can't handle it all, we establish a way to filter through it all and decide what to save. The decisions made by that filter are crucial to who you are.

That filter in the brain is called the reticular activating system (RAS). The way you talk to yourself helps decide what the RAS lets through and the amount of importance it will be assigned. If you say, "I always play the twelfth hole badly" often enough, that will become your "truth." We are not saying you should say, "I always play number twelve great," because that is not the truth. But you can say: "On number twelve, I will swing with perfect tempo and hold my finish." That would be way more useful.

There are only two categories of information that get through the RAS filter. The first is information that is valuable to you right now. You never noticed all those car ads until your car broke down and you needed to buy a new one. Now those ads seem to be everywhere. You notice them.

The second category is information that alerts you to an imminent threat or danger. Initially when you played the par-3, you hardly noticed the water that hugs the right edge of the green, and you made a par. But then you hit three balls into the water, and now the pond looks like an ocean when you stand on the tee. Your self-talk obsesses on the water, and so your RAS makes you focus on the potential danger. When you step up to hit your tee shot, all you are thinking about is the water and not your decision about the shot, to which you need to be totally committed. You can imagine the results.

That voice shouting inside you programs the RAS to see the world in a certain way. That's why you need to take ownership of your self-talk. To create a positive program inside of you, you need to talk to yourself in a positive way, or at least in a neutral or factual way. The past doesn't have to be your future. Here's the deal: Your self-talk has a direct impact on your performance, and we all have self-talk. We can't change those two realities. But what we can do is learn how to manage self-talk. **Thoughts create feelings and feelings create behavior patterns. When you think something often enough, it becomes your reality.**

There are five kinds of nonproductive self-talk to avoid. They all undermine your ability to be totally present when it is time to perform in the Play Box:

1. **Focusing on the past or future.** Don't think about the poor chip on the last hole or the demanding tee shot coming up three holes from now. Play this hole; hit this shot.

2. **Focusing on outcomes.** Don't add up your score until it is time to add up your score. Don't think about how others are going to judge your performance.

3. **Focusing on things that are not under you control.** So what if your playing partner is annoying? So what if it is starting

to rain? You can't control those things. Focus on what you can control—like keeping your focus.

4. **Focusing on what you are not good at or demanding perfection from yourself.** Play your game with your skills and you will perform to your potential.

During a round, each time you notice nonproductive thinking creeping into your inner monologue, write a note that includes which of the five categories the thinking belongs to. We have two strategies for managing self-talk. The first is to learn how to quiet your mind. This is a skill you can practice. You can learn to be present in the Play Box without thoughts. But if you can't quiet your mind, that's where the second strategy comes in. This strategy has two components: You can distract the mind by humming, singing, counting or some other activity; or you can learn how to manage the voice. This requires that you analyze your self-talk and learn its nature. Do you have a tendency to whine and feel sorry for yourself? Take notes on how you talk to yourself and read them over. Challenge your self-talk. Ask, "Is that true?" Get rid of words like "should" and "must" and "need to." You write the script for that voice inside you.

The way you talk to yourself is important, but so is what you choose to talk about. How many times have you sabotaged a good round by letting your mind race ahead and think something like: "Gee, if I play the last five holes two over par I will break 80"? Or have you lost your focus by remembering a bad shot from the past? Other pitfalls include thinking only about the outcome of the shot rather than the process and sabotaging yourself with an unreasonable demand for perfection, or letting your mind obsess on factors beyond your control, like the annoying behavior of your opponent.

Since a round of golf lasts more than four hours, it is impossible not to have self-talk pop up at some point. In some stressful situations, an effective short-term solution is to simply distract the self-talk. We've had great success with this. Brittany Lincicome sang to herself between shots when she won the 2009 Kraft Nabisco Championship, and so did Yani Tseng when she captured the 2010 Ricoh Women's British Open. Song-Hee Kim constantly said to herself: "Vanilla yogurt." Kevin Streelman simply asks himself, "Where is the target?" Annika Sorenstam would say, "Fairways and greens, fairways and greens." What are you going to use as a distractor, if needed?

Pia Davis was at home in England watching golf on TV when she heard Mickey Walker, a great player who had become a commentator, mention that Suzann Pettersen had started winning tournaments "after she began working with Lynn Marriott and Pia Nilsson." Pia Davis quickly did a Google search and found our first book, and that started her on her VISION54 quest.

"I read it from cover to cover, getting really excited, including reading long passages out loud to my patient husband," said Pia, who plays to an 8 handicap. "Then I found that Lynn and Pia did programs—and I found a way to get to one in Arizona." And what she found at our school was the Essential that had the greatest impact on creating a peak-performance state for her in the Play Box.

"I learned that golf is much less about 'the result' and much more about how I manage each shot and manage myself during the round," Pia says. "It is not easy. I find I have to be quite disciplined to manage myself for a complete round."

Pia worked on managing her self-talk by concentrating on being neutral in her reaction after disappointing shots. She learned breathing exercises that helped her silence the voice of doubt or anger that would pop up inside her, and she became aware of her tendency to feel victimized by her play.

One way Pia learned to manage her self-talk was to write down the negative things she said to herself and figure out how to rephrase what she said in a more positive way. "Another important one for me is to keep asking, 'Is that true?' when dealing with issues," she says about a self-talk management skill. "I have to say that this is all a work in progress," Pia continues. "The more I work on these concepts and skills, the more there is to discover and then work on further. Pia, Lynn and the team are all incredible people. They are genuinely committed to helping people fall back in love with playing the game of golf."

We asked Pia Davis for an example of how she edits her self-talk, and she told us about a long par-4 hole at her home course. Pia said she would find that voice inside her saying she needed to hit a great drive on this hole and hit the green in two strokes in order to have any chance of making a par. What she learned to do through developing an understanding of self-talk was to rewrite her inner monologue to where she was saying: "I have gotten up-and-down for par on this hole recently, so it is just not true that I have to be on the green in two strokes. In fact, the second shot is more important than the drive because there are times when it is a better strategy to leave my approach shot short and in the right place for a better angle for the chip to the pin. Besides, this is a great driving hole! It is huge and wide open!"

Long-term, it is about creating productive self-talk. Many people simply do not know what their self-talk is like. A good way to start is to say to yourself aloud what that voice inside you says during a round of golf. Write it down and look it over. Is that the way you want to talk to yourself? Instead of being overrun with negative thoughts, happy golfers have habits that allow them to respond more easily from their higher brain center, the neocortex. **From all of our experiences, we have found the most successful and the happiest golfers don't believe everything they think.**

These happy golfers are more skeptical of their negative thoughts. They question the alarms and override them when necessary. They don't fight with their negative thoughts. They know that these are often just by-products of their negativity bias and that they can go beyond the mind and let the thoughts go. **Successful golfers register their positive thoughts more deeply and savor their positive experiences more intensely.**

You can create a mantra that drowns out self-talk. You can create a distractor to the distractor. Once the self-talk starts in a bad direction, it creates a loop that is difficult to escape. You literally talk yourself into poor play. Don't let that happen. Recognize it and replace it. You control the noise. **You don't have to listen when that voice has a prophecy of doom and tells you that you can't do something.**

"I constantly remind myself of a playing focus that is positively stated and specific," Debra says about the way she silences those voices. One mantra that she repeats to herself is: "What you want can be under your control." She also uses the title of our first book to control her self-talk. "The fact that 'every shot must have a purpose' keeps you present."

This is all about taking control and deciding the soundtrack for your life. You get to be both the composer and the singer. Brainwashing is nothing more than repeated self-talk. That's perhaps the most negative way in which self-talk exists. Your entire perception of reality can be changed if you are repeatedly told the world is different from the way you are seeing it. This is how people can be manipulated by fear into acting against their own best interests. That is the way cults work. But you have the opportunity to create whatever cult you want. You can create the cult of great golf.

When we are young, others determine our self-talk culture. Jack Nicklaus grew up in an "Attaboy!" culture. He was constantly told: "You can do it." So was Tiger Woods. Not everyone is as fortunate. But as we become adults, we have the power to alter the self-talk culture surrounding us. If you lacked positive reinforcement as a child and are shadowed by constant doubt, you can change that. **Self-talk is the power train of your thoughts. You have to get hold of it, or it is running you.**

Talk to yourself about things that are under your control. Write down productive self-talk sentences. We all have a tendency to surrender to what Dan Baker called a VERB culture in his book *What Happy People Know*. What do we mean by this? It is the phenomenon that when something bad happens, we run from the responsibility for our actions. Here's how we distance our self:

Victim: I get all the bad breaks.

Entitlement: I deserve better out of life.

Rescue: I want to hit the lottery rather than work to get rich.

Blame: I am not responsible for the situation I am in.

Victim, Entitlement, Rescue, Blame—VERB. Debra had all of these tendencies rattling around in her mind, and for good reasons—reasons that extended far beyond golf.

Her life was going through a major restructuring, and VISION54 helped provide her with the tools she needed to get through it.

"The fears I had about golf shots that used to overcome me were nothing compared to the fears of losing my life," Debra says. "Although I tried to play competitively while going through radiation and chemotherapy, I realized that people let golf get in the way of their spirit, mind, body and soul. Their performance state is compromised by the shots they might not take, not the shot that is presented to them at the time. They live golf, not life."

That is an important realization. Life is lived right now. And that's how golf must be played. Right now. Debra learned to focus on what is going on this instant, and not on what might be or could be or should be. Debra left our school with a full toolbox of skills. Dreams are great motivators for the future, and regrets about the past can be learning devices, but to achieve peak performance, you have to be right here, right now.

"Their teachings are about life, and golf is just the beneficiary," says Debra about VISION54. "Pia and Lynn are life where there is fear. They are hope when there is none. They breathe, live and exude pure potential. I left them with a heart filled with promise, love, joy, imagination and belief in the possibilities of life and golf."

You can actively create a non-VERB culture by learning to manage your self-talk. You can replace a VERB culture with a GOLF culture.

G: Gratitude for the Game. Pay attention to what you do that is Good and Great.

O: Opportunity. Every shot is an Opportunity. The next shot might be your greatest.

L: Love the game and let it make you Laugh.

F: Fun and Focus will make you perform better.

Research conclusively shows that peak performance is more likely to occur when there is no self-talk with you in the Play Box. This state very rarely happens naturally, but you need to learn how to reach that state in the Play Box to play your best golf. We are asking for something very simple from you: Be fully engaged with your mind and body for just a precious few seconds, with no self-talk and no to-do list. Those athletes who do reach such a level describe eerily similar states that are virtually out-of-body experiences: a basketball shooter who can't miss; a baseball hitter to whom the ball appears to be the size of a pumpkin; a golfer who doesn't even remember the sensation of swinging the club and for whom the cup appears to be the size of a trash can.

The time between your Play Box experiences is inevitably filled with self-talk; sometimes you have a debate involving an entire committee raging in your head. We will have that noise in our head as long as we are on this side of the grass. And in golf, self-talk is even more of a challenge than in

other sports because you have so much time between shots—
the vast majority of the time you are on the golf course—in
which that voice has an opportunity to speak to you. Learn
how to make friends with that voice.

"Believing in possibilities has transformed my life and
game," says Debra. "Before, my mind would wander. **Now I
decide, commit and play.** The teachings of Pia and Lynn are
such that they recognize the power of mind over body. One of
the greatest lessons I have learned is that if you take the time
to find out what thoughts lead your game astray, you can pull
out your VISION54 toolbox and create DHEA. I even write
DHEA in purple on my glove to remind me of the positive."

Debra attended our school twice, and after the second
session, she had her best year ever as a competitor, winning
her club championship and several statewide and regional
tournaments. Her handicap fell to 5.5. "The competition was
stunned," Deba said, "and when they asked me my secret, I
told them VISION54."

There are many ways to deal with self-talk. For one, when
you hear that voice, learn how to get back to being present
to the task at hand, which is hitting the golf ball. Look at the
golf ball and talk to it about the journey it is about to embark
upon. Listen to the sounds of nature all around you and make
those the sounds in your mind rather than that voice. Feel
your breathing; listen to your heart; imagine the ball rolling
into the cup. When that voice tries to take your mind off the
shot you are about to hit, sing to it; hum a tune or talk to

others. We know a player who will toss a ball in the air and catch it between shots so his mind focuses on catching the ball rather than on his self-talk.

Why do you think a monk chants during meditation? The repetitive sound quiets the mind. Tension and fear are held at bay by the sweet sound of nothing. A quiet mind is capable of greatness, capable of achieving peak performance.

"The VISON54 tools are with you everywhere and all you need is to go with the journey," says Debra. "It is the journey, not the destination. Every time I struggle with the tendencies that lead my game astray and tighten up, I think of my time with Pia and Lynn and I believe in the possibilities."

While changing your outlook will change the nature of your self-talk, developing a playing focus that is under your control will distract you from that voice inside you. Question that voice; challenge it. Hear your best friend's voice inside you, encouraging you. Create your own "Attaboy!" culture and take it with you wherever you go. You never have to lose an argument with that voice inside you again.

SELF-TALK EXERCISES

1. To have a quieter mind:

- For one minute, feel your breathing.

- For one minute, in your mind's eye see your ball roll in the cup from three feet.

- For one minute, grip a club, close your eyes and feel

your hands on the grip. If you get distracted by your self-talk, start over.

- For one minute, look at an object such as a tee or a golf ball. Can you stay curious the entire time without having a conversation with yourself?

- For one minute, listen to the sounds around you.

- For one minute, count your breaths.

- Be silent for an entire practice session. Don't talk to other people or comment on your own shots. Total silence. Also challenge yourself to have as much inner silence as possible. If you start talking to yourself, what are the tools you can use to silence the voice?

2. To become aware and to create the self-talk you want:

- Write down what you want to believe in order to be a confident person and golfer.

- For an entire practice session or a round of golf, stay aware of your self-talk. Keep ten tees in your right pocket. Every time you notice an unproductive thought, move one tee to the left pocket. Can you finish a practice session with all ten tees still in your right pocket?

- Write down three positive statements you believe about yourself as a golfer.

- Pay attention to your self-talk during the practice session. If you notice a thought that is not productive, replace it with one of the positive statements about yourself as a golfer.

- On the course, notice how you talk to yourself for three holes. Write down those words or use a tape recorder.

- Write down ten self-talk sentences that you would like to have as your inner monologue. Keep reading the list and sense what it feels like inside of you.

- Write down three goals for your golf.

- Write down three beliefs you have that support your goals.

- Write down three self-talk sentences that support the goals and beliefs.

Functional Self-Talk: You can catch yourself having negative or unproductive self-talk and rephrase it.

Masterful Self-Talk: All of your self-talk during a round is productive. You are present with no self-talk or instruction to yourself in the Play Box.

CHAPTER 10

The 2 Practice Essentials

"The secret is in the dirt."

Ben Hogan, who invented practice

SWING KEY: You get good at what you practice.

The 8 Essential Playing Skills for Peak Performance are the tools you need to play your best golf now. The 2 Essential Practice Skills will maximize your return on practice time. Together, they will help you lower your scores. And, just as there are many myths to overcome about playing the game, there is a mountain of misconceptions about how to practice the game, some of which will actually inhibit your development as a player. Hitting golf balls until your hands bleed is only beneficial if you are trying to get a Band-Aid endorsement deal.

Practice needs to be about quality, not only quantity. And it needs to be about golf. The more we have worked as instructors, the more we have become fascinated with the fact that a lot of players spend a lot of time on the practice range with little to show for it. They spend hours hitting golf balls, but they don't get any better at golf. They may develop beautiful, textbook swings, but they don't get the ball in the hole any faster. And the last time we checked, that's the point of the game.

When we recognized this phenomenon, we directed our energy toward more efficient practice. What were the mistakes being made by all those practice junkies who can't translate hitting the ball better on the range to lower scores on the golf course? We found that there are Essential Skills for practice, just as there are for play. **The key concept that we latched onto is the absolute necessity of tearing down the wall between practice and play.** They are both golf. Immerse yourself in the totality of the game.

The main thing you are trying to do is to play better golf on the golf course—not hit the ball great on the practice range. To accomplish that goal, you need to focus all of your attention toward playing on the golf course. When you can't be on the golf course, you have to make your practice as golflike as possible. If you are working on your tempo, for example, you have to pay full attention to that activity—no multitasking allowed—and you have to bring the tempo exercises into real-golf situations, either on the course or in simulated golf on the practice range.

So the first Practice Essential is about making your practice as much like real golf as you can. We call it Simulated Golf. All research says that what you practice is what you get good at. If you practice with chopsticks, you get good at eating with chopsticks. If you practice hitting two dozen 7-irons in a row from a perfect lie, you get good at that. If you practice being unfocused, you get good at that. The point is, if you want to be good at golf, you need to spend at least half your time practicing within the context of the game.

Why do you hit the ball so well on the range and then hit it all over the place when you get on the golf course? Because you have practiced hitting balls on the range. You haven't practiced hitting balls under real playing conditions. There are shot situations and pressures on the course you won't find on the range—unless you intentionally create them. You have to be proactive and change the very essence of how you practice. This is under your control.

The second Practice Essential is to know how to integrate different skills. The three keys to integration are *engagement*, *repetition* and *accurate feedback*. Anytime you want to improve on a small piece of the game—let's say it is your tempo—you need to practice in such a way that you can integrate the improved skill into your game. What is the purpose of your practice? *How* you practice determines what you retain from that practice session and establishes how successfully that knowledge transfers to the golf course. Remember the chapter on storing memories? The practice won't get filed away in your mind if you are not emotionally connected to it. You won't hardwire the new habits, and that's what you are trying to do. Don't scrape and hit; instead, think and hit, feel and hit, learn and hit.

"Most players don't get the best return on investment for their practice times," says Scott Dickson, director of golf at Shaughnessy Golf and Country Club in Vancouver, Canada, who has attended our school several times, both as a player and as a coach. "In this busy world, they need to make practice more efficient. I feel many of these practicers would have more fun and be better off playing the game as opposed to wasting time on the practice range."

If you practice being a great practice range player, that's exactly what you will become. **To practice only on the range is like working on your volleyball game hoping to get good at tennis**. "For you to improve and perform well under the stress of golf, you *must* make practice more like golf," says Scott, who heard about VISION54 at various PGA seminars. Through his experience, Scott knew most players weren't getting much out of practice. At our school he learned why.

Let's look at the first Practice Essential. When you practice on the range, you need to simulate golf. What do we mean by this? We mean, don't just stand there and mindlessly hit golf balls. Is that how you do it when you are playing a round of golf? Of course not. On the golf course, every shot is different, every shot produces a new challenge, and every shot is a new adventure.

How can you create that situation on the practice range? Change clubs for every shot. Change targets. Do your pre-shot routine for every shot. Create pressure by imagining competitive situations. Be very specific in the situations you simulate. Imagine you have a one-stroke lead and have to hit the green and two-putt. Imagine the wind is blowing against you and you have to decide between a 5-iron and 6-iron. Play an imaginary round on the range.

You can also invite things that distract you into your practice. Create a slow-play situation or hit balls with people milling around you and talking; don't give yourself a perfect lie. Don't practice only in perfect situations. **Make your mind recalibrate for each shot you hit on the range.** Hit half shots. You need to practice the real deal. We call this "Bring It On" practice.

"I use a lot of awareness exercises with my students that help them both physically and mentally," Scott says. "I also empower them to coach themselves, learn what makes them 'tick' as players and build on their strengths. That kind of learning stands the test of time on the course—holds up to the challenges of golf—better than just dishing out technical info." Scott has created a learning situation for his students that is focused and thus fruitful.

You can summarize the Practice Essentials with this three-word framework: Real. Wide. Deep.

Real: Practice as if you were actually playing golf.

Wide: Ensure that you are preparing all of the elements of peak performance: the physical, technical, mental, emotional, social and spiritual elements of the game. Cross-training is essential. Address the whole golfer.

Deep: Stay focused and pay attention to your intention. Why are you practicing? What is your intent? You must be 100 percent present. To store positive practice memories you must be fully engaged in the process of practice.

Andy Fish began teaching golf in 1990 and he learned about our VISION54 program while he was at Bob O'Link Golf Club in Highland Park, Illinois, through a friend and member who had taken our program. "I was interested immediately because of my interest in psychology, my undergraduate major, and a need to improve my thinking on the course. I soon found out after participating in a VISION54 school that it is much bigger than thinking on the course. It completely changed the focus of my teaching."

Andy came away from our school much more aware of the need to focus on the whole golfer in his teaching. "Before VISION54, I focused on making the mechanics of all my students better," Andy said. "I now look at the student as a golfer on a journey, and I am here to help them on *their* journey. I look at the whole picture. Now I know that I am a guide to help them enjoy golf. With this thinking I am helping my students more than ever."

Andy told us about a woman he worked with who was a 25

handicap and was not enjoying golf. She worked hard at hitting balls and was getting pointers from her husband. One day she participated in a free clinic taught by Andy that focused on the Think Box. "We needed to make it a clean (mentally) and comfortable place," Andy said. "This change in thinking not only was successful in lowering her handicap to 20 and giving her two new record-low rounds, but she also loves to play golf now. She really enjoys the whole process, from getting ready to play to lunch after. She now owns her journey."

Andy says the most common mistake he sees in the recreational golfer is the obsession with trying to fix things. "They hit a shot to the right and they try to fix it; the next shot is fat and they try to fix it," Andy says. "The player ends up micromanaging their game and never focuses on one thing long enough to improve. I work really hard with my students to help them understand their swing and focus on the one thing that will most benefit them according to their journey." There has been a lot of research done on practice in various disciplines, and we have applied that research to golf. We have simplified all of the research available into the Practice Essentials. The method we have developed works not only in golf but in any skill you are trying to master. A skilled pianist doesn't play the same note over and over. They practice real playing. Why should you hit the same shot over and over? If you honor these Essentials, you can make any practice session effective. It doesn't matter if it's for ten minutes or eight hours.

The first thing you must remember is that to make practice beneficial, you have to be completely engaged in what you are doing. That means you aren't listening to music on an iPod or chatting with the person hitting balls next to you. **To make a new skill become a new habit, you need to pay full attention to the intention of your activity.** If you want to improve your grip, you need to do many repetitions fully focused on the grip, while giving yourself accurate feedback about how you are doing. If you are practicing your balance, we want you to do exercises that provide you feedback on balance. Keep it clean and simple. This is true no matter which component you are working on: Grip, Posture, Play Box, Decision and Commitment, etc.

And remember this: When you practice one piece of the puzzle—like the grip—put it back into the full puzzle as soon as you can. Put it back in the game. Practice the grip every opportunity you have, even at home, but eventually you have to place it into Simulated Golf—you have to practice with your full routine using the new grip and hitting different clubs to different targets. And you need to take the new grip out onto the course.

To be good at golf, you need to learn to perform with the skills you have. **With any piece of the game, you want to learn and create a new habit—a neuropathway in the brain—so you need repetition plus accurate feedback plus engagement.** Let's say you tend to take the club back too far on the inside and you are trying to get back on plane.

How do you create a new habit? You do it by practicing the new move.

View it as if you are going down a snowy hill with your sled. When you make the "new move," you create a path down the slope with your sled. If you stay aware and focused, you can go down the same path many times. After a while, a strong rut has formed and the sled will not go off the path: The new move has now formed as strong a rut as the old move had. In terms of what is happening in your brain, this is called "myelination"—when a protein forms around the neuropathway to ingrain the skill.

But if you go down the slope and you are not focused and are not giving yourself accurate feedback about the new move, you will end up with twelve detours to the main path. When you go out to play, the club will not follow the path you desire. That's why you should never embark on a swing change unless you have the time to commit to it. Under pressure, the most hardwired neuropathway will win out. The old swing will return. You might understand what you are supposed to do, you can see it on a video, and you might have done it many times during a lesson or practice time, but it's not yet hardwired to show up under competitive playing conditions.

Think of it this way: You have a certain foot you like to start with going down stairs—we all do. Let's say it's the right. Now you make a "swing change" and switch to starting with the left foot. You practice this for some time. Then someone yells, "Fire!" Which foot do you think you will use? Of course, the one you are the most familiar with, the one that is most hardwired. That's the swing that will show up under pressure.

Repetition of a specific skill creates repetitive connections in the brain. These repetitive connections, along with accurate feedback and full engagement, trigger cells that produce the fatty insulation called myelin. Myelin insulates the connection, making it fast. The connections get optimized, making them more like a broadband Internet connection than dial-up. You go from understanding the skill to performing the skill without thinking about it.

Ben Hogan's neural pathways with a 5-iron turned into a superhighway. Ben loved to hit balls. Unfortunately, he did not like to putt. Ben's neural pathways for the putting stroke, combined with his negative self-talk about putting, created a less than optimal putting performance. Ben myelinated his 5-iron to an extremely high level. We think that's what he meant when he said the secret is in the dirt. Had Ben known about myelin, he might have spent more time practicing his putting and myelinated his stroke in a more beneficial way.

Essentially, this research concludes that the most productive practice simulates real-game situations. Pilots use a simulator, so do surgical students. Actors have dress rehearsals and previews in front of live audiences before opening night, and sports teams hold scrimmages against other teams. There are some things that can only be learned in actual game situations. Golf is no different.

If you hit dozens of 8-irons from perfect lies and without a target or a routine, you get good at that. But that only helps you on the golf course when you have a shot from a perfect 8-iron distance and from a perfect lie and with multiple attempts. And how many times a round does that happen for you? Wouldn't it make more sense to practice a three-quarter 8-iron from a bad lie after you have hit a tee shot at a specific target? Make it real golf!

It is so easy to let bad habits seep into your routine. **If you hit shots on the range while talking to others, without your mind engaged, you are not practicing golf; you are practicing being unfocused.** If you do not have a purpose for your practice, you will actually be hurting your game. Ask yourself: What do you want to be good at? You should never let less than half of your practice time be simulating the real deal. This also makes practice more fun. Make practice part of the game and not a separate component of it.

"I believe that to continue to grow the game and grow the number of players, fun should be the number-one ingredient," says Scott. "VISION54 taps into this and allows players to play the game in a way that they have never understood before. I have seen countless students get more out of the game and drop those handicaps without delving into the mechanical, technical world of the game, though there is definitely room for that element."

Most players use the word "work" to describe practice. You can change that. You can make it "play," and in doing so, make it more productive. If you don't have time to play eighteen holes or even nine holes, play on the range. Use our exercises to have fun and learn. And remember this: **Only practice for as long as you can be present and engaged.** If your attention starts to wander, take a break or stop. Don't practice bad habits.

There will be times when you have to focus your practice on just a small piece of the game, such as turning differently in the backswing. At these times you are not practicing golf anymore—you are trying to develop a detail of the game. The key here is to put the component back in simulation and in real-golf situations as soon as possible. You might practice the turn you want for fifteen minutes with accurate feedback and then go back to simulating golf with the new move.

Butch Harmon always said one of the amazing things about Tiger Woods was his courage to take new things he had learned right out on the golf course. That is a sign of confidence, but it is also recognition that only in real-golf situations does real learning occur. In fact, as Tiger was going through his personal crisis during the 2010 season, he was also trying to make a swing change that would allow him to be more consistent off the tee. Even though he struggled, Woods kept playing, knowing real improvement would only come in real-golf situations. He also was willing to accept the fact that he would get worse before he got better.

This is an important fact to be aware of. If you want to make a swing change, do you have the necessary time to invest in the process? You can't change your swing the day before a tournament or during warm-up. You can make small adjustments, like alignment or the position of the ball in your stance, but you are not going to be able to change the dynamic motion of the swing easily—or quickly. **The trap of over-tinkering is a black hole into which many golfers fall.** If you are a weekend golfer and don't have hours to practice, what is the most efficient way you can get better? A good place to start is with the 8 Essential Playing Skills.

Important rounds don't wait to come along when all the pieces of your game are in perfect shape; they come when they come. You always want to know how to play with what you've got. You can practice being prepared for this, but only if you make practice like golf and pay attention to your intention. With those Essentials, your practice will be much more productive and will lead you to lower scores.

SIMULATED GOLF EXERCISES

- Play as many imaginary holes as you can in thirty minutes on the practice area. Imagine the course and your playing partners. Hit the clubs in the order you would hit them on the course. Take breaks between shots.

- Imagine you are leading a tournament by four strokes with three holes to go. Play the last three holes.

- Hit ten shots in twenty minutes. Imagine each one having a specific, important meaning. What is your strategy for managing your emotional state before stepping into the

Think Box and the Play Box? What percentage of shots did you hit the way you wanted to?

- Imagine each of these situations and hit the shot:

    Hit a 6-iron to a par-3 with the pin fifteen feet from a bunker.

    Hit a sixty-yard pitch shot against a 30-mph wind.

    Hit a punch 9-iron between two trees four yards apart and twenty yards in front of you.

    Hit a drive around a dogleg with a slight draw.

    Hit a super-high hybrid over some trees ninety yards in front of you.

- Make four chip-and-one putts in a row. Make each chip different.

- Make ten consecutive three-foot putts from different locations. Do your full routine.

- Putt six different twenty-footers with the goal of getting the ball to the hole or a maximum one putter length past the hole.

- Make ten consecutive three-footers from a circle around the hole.

- Chip from the same spot with four different clubs—sand wedge, pitching wedge, 9-iron and 8-iron. Do this until you get all four shots within a club length of the hole. When finished, repeat the same drill to another hole.

- Set up a five-hole course around the chipping green with the par being 10. Play as many rounds as you can in thirty minutes.

- Invite distractions to a practice session. Have someone talk during your swing or place a shadow across your line or jingle change in a pocket. Can you stay engaged in your Play Box even when distractions occur? Earl Woods would do this with his son when Tiger was a child.

- Place gloves, head covers or anything you can find at ten-, twenty-, thirty-, forty-, fifty-yard intervals and as far as you can go. Hit pitch shots at the different distances. Mix it up for every shot.

CHAPTER 11

Know Your MY54 and NOT54

"Be yourself, everyone else is already taken."

Oscar Wilde, Irish writer and poet

SWING KEY: Golf is predictably unpredictable. The only constant is you.

The VISION54 approach evolved from a very specific concept of how to reach a peak-performance state on the golf course. When Pia was coaching the Swedish national team, she would ask her players if they had ever birdied the first hole on their home course. Invariably, they had. They were good players. Then she would ask the same question about every hole. When she had finished, she would smile and say, "What fun, you've birdied every hole on the course at one time. Now why not make it your goal to birdie them all on the same day?"

To make eighteen consecutive birdies on a par-72 course would be to shoot a 54, so that became the vision—

VISION54. In many ways, our approach embraces the phenomenon that surrounded the four-minute-mile barrier in track. Many in the sport, and many in science as well, believed it was impossible for a human being to run a mile in under four minutes. Then Roger Bannister broke the barrier on May 6, 1954. Just forty-six days later, John Landy went even lower, and on August 7, they both ran a mile under four minutes in the same race. By the end of the twentieth century, the record was nearly seventeen seconds below the "unbreakable" barrier.

To a far greater extent than most people realize, what you achieve is affected by what you believe you can achieve. In golf, 60 is the magic number. Very few players have gone below it in competition. But when someone shoots 59, that makes 58 seem possible, and when someone shoots 58, that makes 57 seem possible. You get the picture. Many of the barriers we perceive as physical or practical are really conceptual barriers. Someday we may have to talk about VISION53!

While it is a very specific concept, VISION54 is also a metaphor. Having a belief that it is possible to birdie every hole is a way to get people to raise for themselves their visions and what they think is possible. In reality, VISION54 varies for everyone, based on ability, experience and other personal factors. If you have never broken 100, the concept of making a birdie on every hole may be too much to take on—for now. But how about making a bogey on every hole and shooting 90—shattering your barrier of 100? It's all about creating a road map to better play, and the first step is always a belief based on vision.

What we are asking you to do is to expand your belief in what is possible for *you*. In doing so, you will formulate your own VISION54 goals and you will develop your own map for how to get there. This is when you make our skills yours. This is when you take ownership of your golf game. For a few minutes every day, imagine how you are when you play your greatest golf. Make it rich and beautiful. Prepare your nervous system for success! How good do you want to be? We can't emphasize enough how important it is to keep on dreaming, even as an adult! The key is to keep looking for possibilities.

To the day she retired, Annika Sorenstam believed she was going to make eighteen birdies someday. She always played with that belief. When she shot 59, she birdied the first eight holes. And even as Tiger Woods struggled with his game during the 2010 season, when asked if he thought he would still break Jack Nicklaus's record of eighteen professional major championships, he responded with one word: "Absolutely."

For both Sorenstam and Woods, their dream, their vision, was the carrot attached at the end of the stick of greatness that they constantly chased. Among the things we have noticed is that this vision of greatness works best when you are feeling it inside you, viewing it with your own eyes as a first-person experience, rather than observing greatness as a third-person experience from the outside. **Close your eyes**

and envision great golf for you. See, hear and feel the putts, the shots, your tempo and your commitment to your decisions. Greatness is a participatory sport, not a spectator sport.

Peak performance is a universal state we can all achieve, but where it takes us is an intensely personal matter, and all of us have our own path to follow. It is all about you. MY54 is your own recipe for how you play great golf. Be curious and pay attention to what you do when you play well. The more intimate you are with your MY54, the more likely you are to create that state more often—or at least come closer to it.

Playing golf without knowing what your MY54 is would be like driving and not knowing where you are going. All of us are unique as golfers, just like our fingerprints and signatures belong to us alone. You can't play golf like Tiger Woods or Annika Sorenstam. You can learn from them, but you can't play like them, because you are not them. You want to learn to be the best you, playing the game of golf.

All of us have unique bodies, different tension levels, personalized tempos and private emotions. You have to learn to structure your golf game around who you are. **The secret to playing well more often is to better understand how you do things when you do play well.** What are you aware of during the putting stroke or the full swing? What do you do between shots? Do you chat or are you in your own world? If you are in your own world, what are you thinking about? What is your tempo? How do you commit to decisions? The greater clarity you have about the 8 EPS, the more in touch you will be with your MY54. How do you warm up when you have your best rounds? What do you eat and drink? Learning and using this information will take you from being a player who happens to perform well a few times a golf season, to being a golfer who can consciously create a state in which good golf occurs more often.

Bob Currey is a successful businessman from Boston who runs his own risk-management consulting firm. He is also a scratch golfer who has won many club championships and competed in some of the most prestigious senior amateur events in the world. At one point, he was ranked number eleven among male senior amateurs in the United States. Bob's relationship with golf is extremely complicated, and by the time he attended one of our schools with his son, his love/hate relationship with the game had tilted toward the negative side.

When Bob started the search for his MY54, he was looking for something far different from what he found. He assumed the bad attitude he had developed about golf had to do with some disappointing outcomes in tournaments—something completely outside his control. But he learned that his feelings about the game were not the result of how he played, but rather how he reacted to how he played. And that reaction is completely within his control.

"Golf has hurt my feelings on a thousand occasions," Bob says, "but I always come back for more. Truth be told, I love the game. Disappointments aside, it has enriched my life." For years, Bob was a solid club player, and then he took on tournament golf and had a lot of very good finishes his first few years of competition. But after a while, the travel and the tension began to wear on him. He also came to another realization.

"I have a confession," Bob says. "For me, competitive golf was never fun. It was work. In fact, it was much worse than work. Unfortunately, I do not hit shots in competition with much joy, only fear and angst. Despite these limitations, I was able to become a very decent competitor." But he was not a happy player. Bob has since greatly reduced his tournament schedule and gone back to playing golf with his friends. Part of his renewed affection for the game comes from the fact that he now better understands his relationship with golf. He realizes that he was letting external forces determine his feelings about the game, rather than asserting control over those feelings himself.

"I am now completely satisfied with my limited competitive accomplishments," Bob says. "Some of that peace of mind can be attributed to a conversation I had with either Pia or Lynn, I can't remember which. She said: **'Only *you* are responsible for *your* attitude about golf.'** That struck a chord with me. If I am in charge and I am a disciplined person, then I ought to be able to have fun no matter the outcome of a tournament or round or even shot. You can't imagine how liberating that mind-set is for a type-A personality like me."

Among the questions we ask players who come to our school is what they want to get out of the sessions. And among the most common answers is: "I want to learn how to be more consistent." When we press them to elaborate on that answer, we usually find that what they mean is that they want to play their best golf more often. We also find that when they think about it, most players realize that they are actually more consistent than they perceive themselves as being—just not always in the way they desire.

A key to playing better is understanding the ways in which you are consistent when you play well. This will lead you to your MY54. Make a list of how you are when you play well:

My legs feel light.

I smile and laugh a lot.

I make clear decisions before hitting.

I start my warm-up by putting.

One of the players we work with came to understand that when she was playing well, she would walk with her head held high and her eyes fixed on the horizon. This was an important realization because she learned that when her game went into a funk, she would look at her feet. She found that she could change her mood—and improve her play—by changing the focus of her eyes from the ground to the horizon. Literally, things were looking up.

Discovering his MY54, Bob Currey reached two conclusions. "Of all the pillars of the game, the one that really matters for me is the spirit of the game," Bob says. "Without that, all the rest is wasted. I left their school committed to enjoying every round of golf no matter how badly I played or how poorly I was treated by the golfing gods. When I see players get angry, frustrated, play the victim or exhibit any of a host of other negative traits, I thank goodness I found those two nice ladies in Arizona."

Now, on the golf course, Bob focuses on improving his attitude. He reminds himself how fortunate he is to be playing golf, and he embraces the sheer joy the game can bring if you are receptive to it. Bob's prime focus now is maintaining that receptive state of mind. He has also changed the way he practices and prepares to play.

"When I was at the VISION54 school, I realized how important the short game is to shooting consistent scores," Bob says. "Now, I spend eighty percent of my practice time around the green. I can hit it sideways and still post a decent score. I aspire to hit serviceable golf shots and great putts. Also, I practice like golf is played. One ball." By concentrating on his attitude—and his short game—Bob is playing great golf again and enjoying it more than ever. He also plays with more self-assurance.

"Good results don't guarantee confidence," Bob says, referring to an element he learned at our school. "Confidence comes from realizing that you can live with your failures, knowing that the sun will still rise in the morning, that your family and dog will still love you and that your golf results do not really matter one bit. I am not defined by my golf scores or my worst swings."

The true test of who we are comes not when things are going well but when we hit choppy waters, as we all do. Some players think they should play MY54 golf every time they tee the ball up. If they don't, they think something is wrong. We want to make sure you don't carry that belief. Any great player will tell you that it is easy to play when you are playing well. Winning tournaments, they will tell you, often has a lot to do with how well you perform on those days when you have not entirely accessed your MY54.

A few times during the year all the pieces of the puzzle are in place. Everything seems perfect. Your swing feels great, your touch is awake, your body feels alive, you are happy, you like the course and who you are playing with. But the reality of golf is that most days are not like that. Something is out of place. There can be thousands of things that upset your MY54. Maybe the pillow in the hotel gave you a stiff neck, or you have worries from work or home. As a result, you can't find the speed on the greens, or your ball flight is a little funky.

It happens to every golfer. The ones who learn to perform the best recognize this disruption early and do something about it. **Just as you are consistent in what you do when you play well, you are consistent in what you do to get in your own way.** We call that your NOT54. You want to be as aware of the ways in which you get in your own way as you are about the things you do when you play well.

Do you get tight in your shoulders, or change your grip pressure, or start being critical of yourself, or stay over the ball longer before hitting? Too many golfers recognize these problems after the round—when it's too late. They might say, "I think I started swinging too fast on the eleventh hole and then I lost it." Write down all the situations that bother you: getting advice from others, arriving late to the golf course, slow play, others watching you, etc. What are you going to do about these situations? Practice them. **Knowing your NOT54 makes you less vulnerable to the tweak of the week or your friends' advice.**

Understanding your undesirable tendencies and having the ability to catch yourself mid-meltdown—your NOT54—is extremely beneficial. When you are able to say, "Aha, here I go again," you can more easily and efficiently get yourself and your game back on track.

Once you know your MY54 and your NOT54, you want to start exploring what tools you can use to shift back toward MY54 when you slip into the NOT54 state. There are countless ways to get back nearer to your performance state, including breathing exercises, stretching, laughing, going to the happy place in your heart, and using a lighter grip pressure. The only way to find out if a state-shifting tool works for you is to use it on the golf course. Keep trying different things until you have a handful of choices.

One of our favorite exercises is to write your strategies for MY54 on a piece of paper. On another piece of paper, write your NOT54 tendencies. Put them on the ground separate from each other and stick a tee through each piece of paper. Read the MY54 note and create that state while hitting shots or putts. Now walk to the NOT54 paper and hit shots or putts while you create the state of getting in your own way. Yes, we want you to practice being "bad." After you have experienced the NOT54 state, move back to "the real you"— MY54—and re-create that state. When you realize you can shift back to MY54, you will have the power to do it on the course. The fancy name for this process is having "paradoxical intentions."

Another great exercise is to write down all the things and situations that bother you—slow play, noise, wind, etc.—then create these situations in your practice. How does each situation alter your MY54 state? Does it change your tempo, influence how present you are in the Play Box, impact the time you take to make a clear decision? What can you do differently to get closer to your best state in each situation? **Knowing your MY54 and NOT54 allows you to manage your state so that you can play your best on *this particular day*, no matter what skill level you brought to the golf course with you on that day.**

Getting to know your MY54 is a process. Keep a notebook in your bag, and for a month keep track of how you feel, behave and play. What patterns do you notice? Are you the same person on the golf course that you are at home or at work? What makes you happy? What makes you angry? How do you react to those emotions? What is there that is consistently present when you play your best golf? You are empowering yourself to control your game, your life and your state on the golf course. That understanding left Bob Currey in a much better place.

"I am more at peace," Bob says. "Results do not define me, effort does. I still try hard in everything I do, but I accept that hard work does not guarantee good results. On my tombstone, they will write, 'He Tried.' That says a lot." The joy, Bob learned, is in the trying. **The joy is in the process.** With that breakthrough, Bob came to realize that he can have a good time and have fun every time he steps on the golf course, not just when he wins or plays well. That's a joy you can experience also.

MY54 AND NOT54 EXERCISES

- Write down your great qualities as a golfer. Ask somebody who knows your game to help with this.

- For three minutes, imagine what it is like to play your best golf. See it, feel it and hear it, the more detail the better. Write down what you experienced.

- Write down the things that you know you do, think, see, feel and hear when you are confident and play well. This is your MY54!

- List what would make sense for you to do in your warm-up to access your MY54 state.

- Write down what you need to believe in order to be a confident golfer.

- Write down the things that you know you do, think, see, feel and hear when you are not confident and don't play well. This is your NOT54.

- Ask someone who knows your game well to list things you do when you play great and what you do when you get in your own way.

- Write down three beliefs that hinder you from being confident as a golfer. Reframe what you wrote so it can be turned into a positive statement about you as a golfer.

- For an entire practice session, have the body posture and presence of a world champion. How would you stand, talk, walk, prepare, focus and commit?

- Write down three tools to use to shift your state from NOT54 to MY54. Use these tools the next time you play. If they don't work, pick other ones and try them. Keep doing it until you have found the tools that work for you.

- Alternate between hitting shots that you are comfortable with and shots that you are uncomfortable with. These can be with different lies, clubs, trajectories or situations. Pay attention and make notes about your Play Box, Decision and Commitment, Balance, Tempo and Tension Awareness for each shot. Any differences? What can you improve on when you hit the "uncomfortable" shots?

CHAPTER 12

Become a Complete Player Now

"Sports do not build character; they reveal it."
Basketball coach John Wooden

SWING KEY: Play your best golf now.

The tools you need to play your best golf are all in this book. These are skills that will complement your technique and make you a player of the game and not just a student of the swing. Like your game, like your swing, like every aspect of your life, they are uniquely yours. And like everything else, the degree to which you will succeed with these tools depends on your commitment to them. VISION54 is not a place where you arrive, but rather a path upon which you travel. Golf is a game you can play your entire life. That is part of its unique nature. These tools are skills for your entire life, and they can last a lifetime—if you commit to making that happen.

To play your best golf now, you must be fully engaged

with every shot you hit. That engagement is not an accident. It is the result of the tools you have learned here. Now you have to put all of that knowledge to work. You must practice with a purpose, you must play with a purpose, and you must do both with a passion. Your toolbox is now full. What are you going to build with those tools? It's up to you to determine the ways in which these tools work best for you.

The 8 Essential Playing Skills are exactly that—Essentials. They are the product of endless hours of interaction we have had with players of all skill levels. These tools will enhance the skills you already have, and they will build upon the unquestionable fundamentals of the game. Proper grip, stance and posture are certainly a necessity, but more is needed for you to be a complete player. The 8 Essentials are fundamental to your enjoyment of the game and your performance. For us, peak performance in golf is a blend of science and art. For so long the art has been implicit, like saying, "Trust it." The essential playing skills make the implicit explicit.

Fortunately, how you choose to be today or for each shot is not predetermined by how you were yesterday, or by your last shot. But that will only become your reality if you decide to take control of the Essential Playing Skills. Many players know they should focus on the process, but they don't really know how to do it. The 8 Essential Playing Skills *are* the process. You need to focus on executing each skill. You need to learn how to do the skill, not just understand the skill. If you focus on how you do each Essential Playing Skill, you are engaged in the process that leads to your most desired outcomes.

Many are fooled by the fact that any malfunction in the traditional fundamentals will always manifest itself in the technical aspect of the swing and/or putting stroke. But this does not mean that technique is where the trouble originated. We hope we have impressed upon you that you can play significantly better without changing your swing. In many ways, the skills we have revealed to you are so fundamental—so essential—they are often overlooked or they are implicitly talked about and not made an explicit part of your game through practice. You can't let that happen. We are not saying that you should ignore your mechanics. We are saying you will play much better if your technical skills are complemented by the 8 Essentials.

We also hope we have impressed upon you the fact that golf is all about the Play Box. That is where the game happens; that is where it is experienced. Everything else you have learned is designed to help create a state of pure engagement when you are in the Play Box. As we said, this is the sacred ground of golf. This is where you celebrate the game. For that celebration to be joyous, you need to reach a state of total engagement and complete commitment. You will figure out what tools work best for you in the Play Box to achieve that peak-performance state.

As for the other Essentials, they are all crucial and necessary, but you will be the person who figures out how to prioritize them in regard to your game. After the Play Box, the order in which the other Essentials appear in this book is relatively random. Arrange them in the way that works best for you. Maybe you go most astray in the Decide and Commit area, or perhaps you have problems with Balance, Tempo and Tension Awareness, Emotional Resilience, Storing Memories or Self-Talk. You should use this book to customize your MY54 and to learn how to manage your NOT54.

Playing your best golf is all about understanding your relationship with the game and gaining a better understanding of how you interact with the game, especially under the pressure to perform. Our suggestion is that you focus on one Essential at a time. Practice that Essential and then take it out onto the course. Keep stats about your performance with any Essential you work on. Create a report card grading yourself from one to five. After getting all of the Essentials to a functional level, you will know which ones need regular maintenance for you and which ones will serve you best in warming up for a round.

The 2 Practice Essentials are simply nonnegotiable. To not follow them is to waste your time when you practice. You will get a good return on investment for the hours you spend on the practice range only if you follow these Essentials: Make practice like golf—simulate the game or practice on the course—and learn how to best integrate the skills you practice into your game. For both Practice Essentials, you want to pay attention to your intention. This makes so much sense, but it is also often overlooked. **You get good at what you practice, so you want to practice golf—not practice practice**.

Your practice must have a purpose or you are ingraining bad habits, especially a sloppy Play Box state. If you just step up and slap the ball in practice, that habit will carry over to the golf course, and you will just step up and slap the ball there. If you have only good lies in practice, how will you handle the situation when you have a bad lie on the golf course? **You can prepare for the unexpected by simulating the unexpected in your practice.** Be creative with your practice. Have fun with it. Create an atmosphere of engagement. Build the positive perspective that will follow you onto the golf course. You shouldn't be afraid to leave the range to go play—you should be excited, joyous, thrilled.

All swing instructors would agree that the game comes down to how you perform when you step up to the golf ball—how you perform in the Play Box. Learning is meaningless unless that knowledge can be put to use when it matters most. We differ with a lot of teachers in that we don't believe that perfecting the golf swing should be the prime focus of instruction; we believe this is putting the cart before the horse. Actually, it is more like putting the horse in the cart. It's not going to get you anywhere. **Golf is a total human experience that is much more complete and much more satisfying than merely the mechanical motions involved.**

Swinging the club perfectly is not the purpose of the game; the purpose is to get the ball in the hole in the fewest number of stokes. You are playing for your score, not to get style points. You don't have to swing it perfectly; you have to swing it well enough. You don't have to have perfect technique; you have to have functional technique: Certainly, you have to grip the club properly, stand properly and rotate properly—but you don't have to do any of that perfectly. **Obsessing over perfection will distract you from your ultimate goal—to play your best golf now.**

Lots of good-enough, some good and a few great shots lead to low scores. We often say you can practice for perfection, but to play successfully, you need to be OK with "good enough" on the course. Are you in good-enough position on the fairway to hit your second shot? Is the shot in a good enough spot on the green for you to have a reasonable putt?

Swing theory is all well and good, and there are many methods of teaching out there that work just fine. And that's the point: There are many swings that work just fine. **There is not one swing that is the best, or everyone would be using that swing. But there is one swing that is best for you, and that is your swing. You have to find it and make it repeat.** At VISION54 we are technically agnostic. We are asking you to take swing theory one step further—recognize and embrace all of the diverse elements that affect technique and performance.

The details of a good swing are only one aspect of the

formula that leads to a happy golf shot. Remember this formula; write it down and embrace it: PTMESS—Golf is Physical, Technical, Mental, Emotional, Social, and your Spirit of the game. You cannot focus on just one aspect—like just the technical—and expect to play your best golf. This is the whole-game approach, remember?

Golf should exist on many levels for you. Make your dreams big; make your goals off the charts; make your vision of the future in the brightest colors imaginable. Make your worldview VISON54. But don't allow it to be just a vision, just a dream. Make it happen. That's the part that is up to you. You can have your goals, but make certain you have a plan for how to achieve those goals. It takes thousands of nails to build a house. The same is true for your golf dreams. But only you can drive in those nails.

To play the game as well as you are capable of playing it, you have to master the game within the game. What is your playing focus today? Is it, "I will finish every shot in balance"? Is it, "I will remain in a good mood no matter how others behave"? Or is it, "I am going to distract my self-talk today by singing to it"? Whatever you choose as a playing focus, it has to be something under your control. And whatever you choose, you have to commit to it completely.

Everybody puts the focus on outcome in golf: What did you shoot? Did you win? But those are things you can't control. You can't control score; you could get bad bounces or the wind could blow. You can't control winning; you can play very well and someone else can play one stroke better. There is no way to control that. So you have to focus on things that are under your control, like the inner game. That is where you create an environment in which the possibility for peak performance not only exists but thrives.

What you focus on will be up to you. What works best for you will be your discovery. It will be your promise, your commitment to yourself. Just make sure it is something under your control. Give your focus a score relating to how much it is under your control, with one representing no control and one hundred representing complete control. Once you are sure your playing focus is under your control, make it specific and state it positively. Your playing focus will enable you to create a state of complete engagement with the game. It will keep you on task.

We are often asked how we feel about goal-setting, and it's a tricky question. Failing to reach your goal can lead to disappointment and a loss of confidence, so goals can be confusing. But it is important, in golf and life, to have a clear vision of what you want to achieve and to understand what aspects of your vision are under your control. Your mind and body need the direction of your goals to function at a high level.

We talk to the players about three types of goals. The first is to imagine what you want to happen. Your nervous system needs to be prepared for success. Imaging greatness is just as important as the physical part of practice. You want to really experience what being great feels like. Dream big; believe that anything is possible and that you can truly be as great as you want to be. Nurture the ability that has been inside you since you were a child. Tap into your full potential in terms of both how you play golf and who you are as a person.

The research is very clear on this: For sustainable performance, the extrinsic (outcome goals) needs to be balanced with the intrinsic (your spirit of the game). Most players only focus on the extrinsic goals, and that can lead to great frustration. You should pursue your goals, but don't let results control your emotions. Love doing what you are doing beyond the outcomes! Conjure up a dream of greatness and paint the details in vivid colors. An important initial step toward greatness is to imagine greatness. Embracing the spirit of a specific goal can be great motivation for achieving that goal.

The second type of goal is more traditional, and it involves outcome, such as lowering your average number of putts per round or your scoring average. This motivates some people and works well for them. Others are the kind of people who can lose their motivation when they don't reach goals of this kind, sometimes within an unrealistically quick time frame.

You should pay attention to how you react to this type of goal-setting. If it helps you, keep doing it; if it doesn't support your progress, eliminate it from your program. One year, Annika Sorenstam decided to improve her bunker play, kept detailed statistics on her performance and ended the year moving from number forty-five in sand saves to number one. This approach works for her extremely detail-oriented approach to golf—and to life! Many other great players are relieved to learn that they don't need to focus so much on these kind of goals. It frees them up.

The third type of goal is what we call "to-do goals." They are the actions you decide to commit to that are 100 percent under your control. It could be: "Today I will exercise for forty-five minutes." Or perhaps: "My focus today will be to swing at eighty percent of full tempo" or "Today I will simulate golf for more than fifty percent of my practice time." Our experience is that we all do well with the first and third approaches to goal-setting. Imagine what you want to be, then set to-do goals that get you there step-by-step.

We can't emphasize enough how important it is to act on the aspects of your game that will improve your performance. When Sorenstam decided to focus on making her bunker play better, it was in large part because there were so few other areas of her game that needed improvement. She identified a weakness and addressed it. Sometimes we even tell our students that they can't come back to our school until they have gone home and done something to move their journey forward.

Go back to the title of this book, *Play Your Best Golf Now*. Let's look at each of those words and see what a beautiful sentence that is.

PLAY: Don't ever forget that this is a game. Nothing that happens on the golf course is going to change your overall life. Even if you are a professional, the most important aspects of your life are off the golf course: those you love and who love you. You should never fear a game. You should enjoy it. No matter your score, the sun comes up and the flowers bloom.

YOUR: Reaching peak performance is a totally personal process. Your peak performance can only happen to you, no one else. And your path for achieving a peak-performance state will also be uniquely yours. Yes, there are the Essentials, but they are the ingredients to the soup, and you will be the chef who determines the proportions that work best for you and suit your taste. You will figure out the recipe for your MY54, and you will understand your NOT54.

BEST: What a wonderful word this is! We don't say "perfect," we say "best." And your best golf is, once again, a completely personal definition. Every principle embraced by VISION54 begins with the foundation that the player is a person first and a golfer second. You are a person who happens to play golf. The meaning of "best golf" not only varies from person to person, but it will vary for you from day to day, round to round. What you have learned here will help you play your best with what you have and who you are on this particular day.

GOLF: What an awesome game we have the pleasure of playing! While all sports require focus and concentration, and while peak performance in any activity has similar requirements to reach that state, golf is a uniquely tranquil activity that embraces the beauty of its surroundings and involves the personality of its participants more than any other. It is a game for life; it is a game about life.

NOW: The dream does not have to be deferred. The way to get better, the way to score lower, is to play the best you can play right now. If you are able to maximize your potential today, perhaps the bar will be raised higher tomorrow. What you can achieve is affected by what you believe you can achieve. Play your best golf now, today, and who knows what you can achieve tomorrow? But enjoy the now; that's where you are living, not in the tomorrow—or the yesterday.

We think one of the fun things about our approach is that it is simultaneously very specific and very improvisational. Our Essentials are like the outline for an ad-lib acting piece. There are components that are necessary—pieces that are the essential parts to the puzzle of playing golf—but we are giving you complete freedom in how you arrange those pieces. **The final picture of your best golf will be drawn by you, not by us.**

We can point out the Essentials and we can help you learn the skills that enable you to master those Essentials, but none of this works if you just read them and understand them. It's all about *doing*, taking action. **All the Essentials are free. You don't need any equipment to become good at them. They live inside of you and are always available.** When will you start using them? Become an actor rather than a reactor. Create possibilities with your swing and your game.

You will Play Your Best Golf Now when you understand your needs in the exciting equation of golf, and then formulate the best strategy for employing the Essentials for you—just as the remarkable people you have met in these pages have done. From them, we hope you have learned this: The Essential Playing Skills work, and they worked for each of these people in very different ways.

They each found their stepladder to better golf in a different place. But they all enjoy golf more now because they learned skills that helped them reach their full potential and enabled them to enjoy the experience of golf more. Now you have the tools to do the same thing—enjoy! It's time for you to Play Your Best Golf Now.

ACKNOWLEDGMENTS

For us to stay on our journey of development, we need inspiration, complex challenges, joy and reasons to go deep with our knowledge and understanding of this glorious game. Our greatest source for this motivation has always been the players we coach. The Pearl, Tutta, BTG, Annika, Braveheart, Grid Master, Nils, Streels, Sari, Jason, Minni, Yuko, Stan, Grace, Rob, Howard, Mike, Kristine, NYC and Tiffany: What do you all have in common? You are all examples of players who have helped form our vision and inspired us to act on that vision.

THANK YOU to all the heroes and friends who have crossed our path in teaching and coaching through the years. We could write an inspiring chapter about each of you. Your performance and enjoyment on the golf course is our scorecard. It is what drives us to get up every day and create exercises and experiences so you can become your own best coach.

The challenges that each and every player brings to our coaching tee makes us think deeper and wider. It's when you are confused or frustrated that we become inspired to do a better job at helping you understand your game more completely or enjoy it more. Sometimes the simplest idea or skill can make the biggest difference.

In our heart of hearts, we want you to Play Your Best Golf Now. It's time to honor the complete golfer in you. It's time to take the mystery out of all this conflicting swing instruction and focus your energy and efforts into skills that will help you play better golf and not just make a better golf swing. Most important is how you take the swing you have worked so hard to groove and make it more functional on the golf course. We want the time, money and energy you spend on your game to yield a bigger return on investment.

Thanks once again, Ron. Your love, friendship and support mean the world to us. We love the teamwork and synergy with you. Thank you for being as passionate about VISION54 as we are.

Thank you, Bill Shinker and Jessica Sindler, for trusting us and guiding us along the journey of getting the book completed.

Thank you, David McCormick and Mark Reiter. In the world of agents, you have been the best. We hope this book helps you play better golf now.

Lynn Marriott and Pia Nilsson
Phoenix, Arizona, and
Torekov, Sweden
2011

Soon after Ben Crenshaw pulled off an emotional victory at the 1995 Masters just days removed from serving as a pallbearer for his longtime coach, Harvey Penick, I asked Ben what he made of the incredible outpouring of affection he received from the fans over the last few holes at Augusta National Golf Club. He told me he felt it was because Harvey's death touched something deep inside each and every one of those spectators. "We all had someone who first put a golf club in our hands," Ben said. "For me it was Harvey. Those people weren't so much cheering for me as they were cheering for the first person who put a club in their hands." That understanding by Crenshaw helps explain his success in the game. Ben always played with his heart. He has had a lifelong love affair with golf.

The people whose stories are in this book have that same emotional bond to golf. I want to thank Major Dan Rooney, Marlo Stil, Walter "Topper" Owen, Ai Miyazato, Barbara Bonney, Stan Freimuth, Vikki Templeton, Beth Brown, Debra Oberg, Pia Davis, Scott Dickson, Andy Fish and Bob Currey for telling me their stories with astonishing honesty and inspiring passion. At the core of the VISION54 philosophy is the understanding that golf is a deeply personal experience through which each individual must find his own path. This dedicated baker's dozen articulated brilliantly how the 8 Essential Playing Skills set their compass on a true course for better play and more fun.

Few people I have played golf with are as passionate about

the game as Bill Shinker at Gotham Books. He is not only supportive and visionary as a publisher, but inspiring for a writer to be around. Jessica Sindler's steady hand and wise insights superbly guided this book through the editing process. David McCormick of McCormick & Williams is everything a writer could ask for in an agent. Thanks to all of you.

This is the third book I have done with Lynn Marriott and Pia Nilsson. I respect them as collaborators, I cherish them as friends, and I believe with all my heart that the game of golf is better because of their enormous contributions. They have taken a game that has been overintellectualized and fragmented into dozens of components and put the pieces back together into a truly human experience. I thank them for allowing me the opportunity to work with them, and I thank them for all they have done for golf.

The golf club was first put in my hand by my father, John Sirak, a steelworker drawn to the game when he was thirty-five years old by a local boy from western Pennsylvania who started winning golf tournaments—Arnold Palmer. My first job in golf was reloading the pop cooler at Castle Hills Golf Course in New Castle, Pennsylvania, each night when I was twelve years old. For that, I could play golf for free, an arrangement my father set up. I thank Arnold for bringing the game to the people, and I thank Dad for bringing me to the game.

Ron Sirak
South Wellfleet, Massachusetts
2011

For further learning about VISION54, go to VISION54 .com. There you will be directed to training and products to support the integration of the Essential Playing Skills and to social media and multimedia options, as well as to sign up for our e-newsletter.